D1516716

WHEN CHANGE FINDS YOU

WHEN CHANGE FINDS YOU

31 ASSURANCES to Settle Your Heart When Life Stirs You Up

Kristen Strong

Revell
a division of Baker Publishing Group
Grand Rapids, Michigan

Published by Revell
a division of Baker Publishing Group
PO Box 6287, Grand Rapids, MI 49516-6287
www.revellbooks.com

Printed in China

Library of Congress Cataloging-in-Publication Data
Names: Strong, Kristen, author.
Title: When change finds you : 31 assurances to settle your heart when life stirs you up / Kristen Strong.
Description: Grand Rapids, Michigan : Revell, a division of Baker Publishing Group, [2021] | Includes bibliographical references.
Identifiers: LCCN 2021003817 | ISBN 9780800738860 (cloth) | ISBN 9781493431922 (ebook)
Subjects: LCSH: Change (Psychology)—Religious aspects—Christianity—Prayers and devotions.
Classification: LCC BV4599.5.C44 S77 2021 | DDC 242—dc23
LC record available at https://lccn.loc.gov/2021003817

21 22 23 24 25 26 27 7 6 5 4 3 2 1

For the military spouses: may you always know that wherever change takes you, God's unchanging love goes with you. You're appreciated and so, so beloved.

Contents

Acknowledgments

Thank you, Father, Son, and Holy Spirit, for your faithful presence, support, and comfort as I've tapped out the words to this book.

To my endlessly kind and good man, David: you've brought a lot of change in my life, but your patience and wisdom in walking through it with me have never changed—and changed me for the better. You're God's best gift to me, and I love you wildly.

To James, Ethan, and Faith: thank you for showing such interest in this project and for all the comic relief when I didn't see how I'd make my deadline. You're the biggest blasts and your Dad's and my greatest treasure. We love you more than you'll ever know, and that will never change.

To Mom, Sara, Chris, Megan, Bev, Lisa, Andy, Kathy, Floyd, AND all my darlin' nieces and nephews: thanks for giving me and the gang fixed places of familiarity and comfort to return home to. You are beloved!

To my #wingwomen who kindly offer their presence in my life and their prayers for this book: Alli, Aimée, Cheryl, Connie, Holley, JulieAnne, Kathy, Kim, Lindsey, Lisa-Jo, Maria, Rebecca, and Salena—thank you. I love each of you more than words can say.

To the Bradley, Crumpton, Leonard, and Powell families: thank you for lifting my family and me up in no less than 752 prayers. You consistently helped carry me through a hard couple of years chock-full of change.

To Aimée: I never want to live in a world without our coffee dates, even when they're six feet apart in an empty parking lot. Thank you for always, always having my back.

To Kaitlyn, my faithful assistant and friend: I'm old enough to be your mama (or at least an older aunt!), but you continually teach me all the new things with such grace. Thank you for all you do.

To Andrea Doering and the posse at Revell: you are just the dearest folks in all of publisherdom. I always get excited when I see an email from you or when I talk with one of you! Thank you for your vision and your faithful support and care. I love you so.

To my agent, Teresa: thank you for your help and expertise!

To every military spouse I've met in person and online: you've consistently and wholeheartedly been a safe place for me, and this book is my small thank you.

To Ellie Holcomb: your song "Red Sea Road" was a constant companion as I wrote this book. Thank you for writing and recording this artistic masterpiece that has been a friend to me during some difficult, heart-wrenching change.

To my porch friends and readers: thank you for loving me as I am, even when I go on too much about cake or country music or not liking winter. You always make a wide-open space for me, and I pray this book offers you a wide-open space to be assured and comforted when difficult change finds you.

Acknowledge

ACKNOWLEDGE THE DIFFERENT LOSSES CHANGE BRINGS.

DAY 1

Simmer Down, Anxiety

The Lord *of hosts is with us; the God of Jacob is our refuge.*
Psalm 46:11 NKJV

My daughter's bloodcurdling scream ricocheted from the garage up to where I sat in my office on the second floor.

I shot out of my chair and sprinted down two flights of stairs. I threw open the door from our mudroom to the garage, calling with no small amount of panic, "Faith! FAITH! Are you okay?!" My bare feet landed on the doormat sitting just inside the garage, just like they'd done a thousand times before. And that's when I noticed a texture under one foot that in no way resembled the doormat. It was soft, kind of squishy. I looked down and in short order let out my own bloodcurdling scream as I realized I had just stepped barefoot—*barefoot*—on a long snake.

I jumped backward, hollering like I was on fire, and shut the garage door between me and it.

After taking a couple deep breaths and giving thanks to God that the creature didn't bite me, I simmered down enough to collect my wits and slowly, gingerly opened the door again. The snake remained in its same position, folded back and forth on the mat like some kind of sadistic ribbon candy. I called for Faith again, and then I saw her waving from the driver's seat of the car parked in the garage. Faith, who had been outside, explained that she had proceeded to walk back toward the house through the same garage door before laying eyes on the snake. That's how she ended up screaming—as she jumped into the car. I looked back at the snake, which hadn't moved a muscle. As riled up as Faith and I had been about the snake, it seemed completely unfazed by us.

After double-checking the snake wasn't poisonous, I began laughing hysterically. Faith, still shut up inside the car, said she wasn't coming out till the snake was long gone.

Dramatic or not, I totally understood that life decision.

Being the tough-as-nails gal I am, I proceeded to ask my sons if one of them would take care of the critter for me. Ethan immediately accepted the job. Like some kind of reptile boss, he sauntered over to the snake, picked it up with his bare hands, and removed it from the premises to the field down the lane.

I tell ya, greater love hath no mama than this, that her sons take care of the bugs and snakes for her. At least, that's the case with me.

Sometimes I view the difficult change in my life—the kind I don't want and didn't ask for—like I viewed that particular snake. I'm walking along, minding my own business, and then this terrible change pops up where I least expect it and my heart immediately drops to my ankles. Or maybe I did expect the change—after all, some difficult change is expected but still unsettling. When that's the case, it can still bring unanticipated surprises.

It may also bring anything from dread to a good scare to major harm. It may bring instant panic or simmering stress. Either way, its unwelcome presence can spin me up and my anxiety right along with it, and it's been doing so since my childhood.

Prone to many an anxious thought as a kid and teen, I can still feel my daddy's arm slung around my shoulders as he said, "Now Kristen, just simmer down, honey. Don't you know God is with you right here, right now?"

I might've been studying for a math test or waiting on the dentist, and he would recognize when I began to panic. My daddy's kind presence reminded me of the Father's kind presence and helped my breathing to slow, my heart rate to calm, and my mind to clear. When I remembered God was near, my anxiety simmered down.

Of course, as the dad of three daughters, he sometimes also told my sisters and me to "simmer down" out of exasperation as we fought over Barbies or baby dolls or who got to sit in the highly coveted front seat of the car. But more often than not, "simmer down" became a gentle touchstone that turned me from the toxic train to truth—and helped my emotions do the same as my reactions to change improved.

I realize you may not be able to imagine having a dad who was a gentle presence in your life. If that's you, I'm so sorry. You deserve to be treasured first and foremost by both your parents. But you *do* have a heavenly Father who treasures you somethin' fierce. If you still yourself and simmer down long enough, you'll sense his closeness saying, *Don't you know I am with you right here, right now?*

God is as next to you as the dining room chair or the snoring husband or the too-empty space at the other end of the couch. And he gave us his Son to be *with us* till the end of time.[1]

I'm past forty-five years old, and how I wish the most anxiety-inducing event brought on by change was a cavity or a pop math quiz. But you don't get to be my age without encountering change that devastates you physically, spiritually, and emotionally.

The writer of Hebrews tells us, "By faith we understand that the universe was created by the word of God, so that what is seen was not made out of things that are visible" (11:3).

If God created the universe from what was invisible, then he can create something beautiful from what you can't yet see in your own life. Don't see how anything good can come from the hot mess you or your loved one is in? Can't make heads or tails of what in the world you're supposed to do next? Well then, buckle your seatbelt, because you're in a prime location to see God make sense of the senseless that sits in your lap.

If God created the universe from what was invisible, then he can create something beautiful from what you can't yet see in your own life.

The road you're traveling may very well have a snake or two stretched across it, and the shock of its discovery may make you scream or run and hide. But hear the Father whisper, *Don't you know I am with you right here, right now?*

Let that speak the message *simmer down* to your anxiety. Dear one, he will resurrect and refashion your devastation into restoration.

Change may come out of nowhere, yes. But wait for the invisible to become visible—it may very well come out of nowhere too.

Dear Father in heaven, I didn't see this change coming, but you did. I know you're not taken off-guard. Right now, I need you like the lifeline you are. As I'm not sure what to think, guide my thoughts. As I'm not sure what to do, be in my actions. As I'm not sure how to make it through, be my strength, Lord. Thank you for your Son, Jesus, who endured the most agonizing change on earth so I could have your unchanging presence. Thank you for being with me always. In Jesus's name, amen.

"My plans keep changing, but I'll keep trusting that perhaps, in these unknowns, my awareness of what really matters will grow."
~Morgan Harper Nichols

God is with you through your difficult change.
When you can't see the good to come out of it, take heart.
He will create something redeemable from the invisible.

DAY 2

Abundance Is Coming

"I will never leave you nor forsake you." So we can confidently say, "The Lord is my helper; I will not fear; what can man do to me?"

Hebrews 13:5–6

No one knows tired like a papa or a mama who's hit 9 PM with a posse of little people in his or her care. A parent could drop right then and there and sleep twelve hours straight, but suddenly the kids are acting like darting hummingbirds who each have a direct line to a sugar IV. They find the mere suggestion of going to sleep akin to you taking away all their birthday presents.

Like every other parent, I've known this exhaustion. I've known the frustration and the irritation that arise as, when a few minutes of elusive peace seem just within reach, your dear but determined little darlings seem bent on stomping all over it. I mean, you've served them all the livelong day by making and hand-delivering three meals plus snacks-times-infinity. You've played no less than 237 games of Candyland and Go Fish and Hi-Ho! Cherry-O. You've maneuvered the tedious balance of giving them roomy play space yet not letting it take over the entire house. You've juggled your work or job while helping them with math that seems awfully complicated for the fourth grade. So, yeah—when bedtime rolls around, you're definitely ready to bid them goodnight-with-a-capital-G.

Several years ago, when my precious wee-watts would come up nightly with 382 ways to stall bedtime, I mentioned an offhand comment to them I'd heard someone else say along the way. Exasperated and just plain *done*, I said, "Listen, after 9 PM, the Holy Spirit leaves my body, and I can't be held responsible for what I might say or do. So, if I were you, I'd get my hind end in bed *pronto* and stay there."

At the risk of stating the obvious, this is *terrible*, *horrible* theology and not true at all. If we're in Christ, we have the Holy Spirit living inside us, period. Still, with my three big kids today—two in college and one in high school—that comment has become a running inside joke, an off-the-cuff remark that stuck. If I start to get cranky late in the evening, I inevitably hear, "Watch out, it's after 9 PM, and you know what happens to Mom after 9 PM!" This isn't to say I don't get cranky before then. Lord have mercy, I sure can. It's just this is what I hear when it happens later in the evening.

Another friend of mine, who happens to be one outstanding mama, uses a similar but kinder, gentler expression for overdue bedtimes. Hearkening to a couple of Bible verses in Lamentations 3, she likes to say, "Remember how we've learned that God's mercies are new every morning? Well, it's late and there are now *no more* new mercies for anyone. Good night and go to sleep!"

I mean, what parent can't relate to that? It's late, we're tired, and we're out of patience. Go. To. Bed.

Yes and amen.

While we mere humans certainly struggle with reaching the end of our rope and running out of resources, God does not. I know this in my head, but sometimes my heart forgets. When a difficult change bursts into my life and interrupts my peaceful existence, my default is to think this change is here because God's reserve of Kristen mercies is all used up. The change moved my circumstances outside of God's care and provision and left nothing but loss in its wake.

It never occurs to me that the change could be a source of God's mercy, not a sign of his indifference.

If I need and want my anxious emotions to simmer down, I need to acknowledge those losses it brings, yes, but also acknowledge that God's love and concern for me extend beyond what I can imagine, and he can bring unimaginable good from this change.

Even if I can't see how.

Even when it seems impossible.

Even though my faith is tissue-paper thin.

A kind reader named Nancy once wrote to me that, regarding her three young children, she struggled to find the middle-of-the-road balance between being too strict and too lenient as a parent. Recalling the wisdom of her own dad, Nancy said that regarding that road, "It's wider than you think." In Nancy's words, that road is a road of grace.[1]

It never occurs to me that the change could be a source of God's mercy, not a sign of his indifference.

As God's children, we travel a road of grace that is ever so much wider than we think, and it leads right up to his heart. No amount of change is going to narrow that road or knock us into the ditch. No amount of change is going to lead us to a dead end, an empty place void of God's grace. His love and faithfulness are the guardrails that assure us of our belonging place on that road.

Yes, change isn't going anywhere, but I do need my typical reaction to change to go away. I need and want to see it with fresh eyes rather than as a lingering wavelength that continues to mess with my equilibrium—or mess with my peaceful evening like an out-of-bed-again kiddo.

When I can acknowledge this change's presence in my life, I can acknowledge it is a grace rather than a grievance, because God uses change like he uses everything else in our lives: to reveal his good plans and purpose for us. Psalm 66 tells us

> You brought us into the net;
>   you laid a crushing burden on our backs;
> you let men ride over our heads;
>   we went through fire and through water;
> *yet* you have brought us out to a place of abundance. (vv. 11–12,
>   emphasis mine)

You're not outside God's concern, not at all. He's not drained his mercies on you already. This change may do its best to crush and overwhelm, but God's mercies for you reach further and higher. Keep going and persevere, for the difficulties come right before the *yet*—

Right before your place of abundance.

Dear heavenly Father, I'm so sorry for the times I act like you dish out mercy like dealing cards and I've got a losing hand. I know that's not true, because your Word says you gave us your Son so we would have the abundant life. I know your mercies are new not just in the morning but also in the afternoon and evening and throughout the night. Help me frame this truth around my change so I can frame myself in a calmer state of heart and mind. Thank you that you redeem everything and make everything new. In the gracious name of your Son, Jesus, amen.

"Often, I think as human beings we are constantly asking God for more. The problem is we don't understand the more he is trying to give us." ~Lisa-Jo Baker

Change is a provision of God's mercy, not his indifference. Part of acknowledging the change in your life is acknowledging it's a grace rather than a grievance, and it will lead you to your place of abundance.

DAY 3

Name the Loss

[God] is unchangeable.

Job 23:13

Do you know what happens when your twin sons leave for college, their little sister has a Texas-sized hole in her heart because of it, and really, your whole house feels positively cavernous without two-thirds of your children within its walls?

Your husband and daughter talk you into getting a new puppy, that's what happens.

Now, you may have serious reservations about adding another four-legged creature into your family. You may have thought now wasn't the best time since, oh I don't know, your sons left for college ten minutes ago. You may think you need just a minute to actually miss them before bringing something new into your life. But you don't say these things out loud. Then your daughter finds a cute puppy from a rescue and she sweet-talks her dad into getting said puppy, and you don't have the energy to fight that kind of megawatt excitement.

So, your family gets the puppy, the same older puppy the rescue told you was "80 percent potty trained." And then the first morning your puppy is under your roof, he decides to relieve himself on the rug you purchased only a month ago. The next several days confirm what you already suspected: this puppy is 100 percent not anywhere in the vicinity of 80 percent potty trained.

You realize too that no matter how often you're told you won't have to care for him (the biggest lie told to mothers since Cain and Abel first asked Eve for a pet), you're the one who gets to train the puppy because you work from home. And when he pees yet again on your new dining room rug, you lose your ever-lovin' mind and consider running up Pikes Peak, screaming like a wild banshee.

Instead, you once again call the carpet cleaning guy who, thanks to this puppy, is funding his child's college education courtesy of you and your thinning wallet.

Certainly, a new puppy wasn't the most life-altering change I was going through. At that time, my sons' move to college filled that role. However, this loss of time and resources piled upon the bigger loss of missing my boys, and I wasn't handling it very well.

Every single change that comes into our lives brings losses, and it's right and good to lament the losses by naming them and giving them space at the table. Unfortunately, I hadn't really done that. Instead, I shoved them to the side right alongside my reservations about getting a dog in the first place.

During this season, the Lord brought me to a garden-fresh awareness of a passage of Scripture I'd never considered before:

> Now there is in Jerusalem by the Sheep Gate a pool, which is called in Hebrew, Bethesda, having five porches. In these lay a great multitude of sick people, blind, lame, paralyzed, waiting for the moving of the water. For an angel went down at a certain time into the pool and stirred up the water; then whoever stepped in first, after the stirring of the water, was made well of whatever disease he had. (John 5:2–4 NKJV)

It's fascinating to read that, for someone to be healed, the waters had to first be stirred up. Not only that, but those who entered into the stirred-up waters only did so because they had faith the healing would come. There is something about things being stirred up that leads to a healing. And isn't change what often stirs things up?

When change shakes the calm right out of our life, healing can come when we step into the change rather than stay away from it. And it seems that in an effort to step into it, a good place to start is to name the losses change brings.

So, in the spirit of naming my own losses, I had an honest tête-à-tête with my husband, David. I acknowledged to him later what I should've acknowledged earlier: I was struggling more than he knew with the boys' absence. All I wanted to do was have the time and space to adjust to that huge change, and I couldn't do that because, as the one at home all day, I was now chief dog caretaker on top of my work and other responsibilities. I didn't really want the dog, and I resented the amount of change it piled on top of an already transitional season.

I also owned that I should've mentioned my struggles sooner, before they reached DEFCON level 1.

Thankfully, David validated my feelings and agreed it was rather thoughtless and inconsiderate of him to bring a new puppy into the house so soon.

(Dang straight and amen.)

After I shared some of this with Faith too, she and her dad came up with a schedule that took some of the pressure off me during the day. Slowly but surely, the dog was housetrained. Slowly but surely, I warmed up to the cute little mutt and was thankful for his presence, which went a long way toward helping our daughter through a difficult time.

I'm still getting used to the loss of parenting three kids full-time at home. But I'm also getting used to naming those losses as they come—and therefore acknowledging this change too.

Whatever the scope of your change, Jesus takes it personally when that change brings you loss. Go ahead and step into the change by lamenting the loss, because the lament acknowledges your honest feelings while also acknowledging the goodness of God.

Stepping into the change brings you one step closer to accepting it.

And stepping into the change brings you one step closer to accepting it.

This change may feel like the end of things, but God will see you through it. Then you'll be able to look at the view in front of you and realize that change is not the end. God's grace and goodness are.

Dear heavenly Father, even when I don't handle things like I should because I've not been honest about my struggles, thank you for your always available presence, attention, and listening ear. Give me the courage to face my struggles honestly and head-on, and give me a safe person or two with whom I can share openly about the loss within my change. Thank you that I don't walk through this change alone—you are my unchangeable companion. In the name of Jesus, amen.

"Jesus's interactions with the people he came in contact with during his life on earth make it clear that desire, and the willingness to name that desire in Christ's presence, is a catalytic element of the spiritual life. . . . Somehow it creates the possibility for Christ to be with us in a way that meets our truest need."
~Ruth Haley Barton, *Sacred Rhythms*

All change brings loss. Go ahead and step into the change by naming the loss for what it is, and remember change is not the end.

DAY 4

Reject the Committee of Internal Critics

But in that coming day no weapon turned against you will succeed. You will silence every voice raised up to accuse you. These benefits are enjoyed by the servants of the LORD; their vindication will come from me. I, the LORD, have spoken!

Isaiah 54:17 NLT

Today, I sit down to a writing routine, hoping the words come before the fear catches up. First I pray, asking God's direction and wisdom for relaying his heart to the hearts of others. Then I sit in my black-and-white buffalo check chair, arranging myself just so. I take a deep breath, put my shaky hands on the keyboard, and type out a few lines. Then, as if some imaginary conductor has raised their baton, a committee of internal critics take their cue to kick things into high gear by criticizing, ridiculing, and rolling their eyes. They read over my shoulder and say things like, *Wow, is that the best you can do? Don't you think people will find out you're a fake who doesn't live up to anything redeemable? Who do you think you are, anyway?* I find myself second-, third-, fourth-guessing what I'm going to say to such a degree it just seems preferable (that is, safer) not to say anything at all. It's easier to go ahead and vacuum the living room or make double chocolate brownies. After all, I like vacuum lines. And making brownies is always the right choice. No fear there.

This problem is compounded by the fact that it's not my first rodeo with fear, not by a long shot.

In one way or another, fear has been a steady companion of mine since childhood. I wasn't born with a lick of natural confidence or moxie, and I felt small and unimportant more often than not. I'm sure I'm not alone in that—perhaps more of us felt this way than didn't. Thankfully, time and maturity and Jesus have helped me deal with a lot of the lies I bought into as a child. I still struggle with fear—it continues to find a place at whatever table I'm sitting. However, it doesn't usually sit at the head of the table, bossing my every move.

Unless it's about my writing work these days.

A while ago, a couple of events occurred to build such a towering bout of fear on the work front that today, once again, I feel thirteen and pretty sure I'm stupid and have nothing to offer but a heaping helping of disappointment. It was as if those events rerouted my heart and brain, making me travel roads I hadn't traveled in years. Surely, I'm small in all the wrong ways and incapable of doing any good through words. I struggle with a real lack of focus, and it has nothing to do with distractions or feeling the pull of social media. It has everything to do with me being nearly incapable of tearing my eyes off fear as she and her critic minions slither back to the head of the table.

The specifics of the change that brought on the fear aren't important. God saw it coming before I did, and since he allowed it, he meant it to be of some kind of help. But what is important is focusing on how I move forward from here—how I don't let the fear change brings keep me going backward.

Because Jesus does not give us a spirit of fear, but of power, love, and a sound mind.[1]

The tricky thing about fear is that it does its level best to push me toward a place of questioning. *What if* this *or* that?

But Christ's love compels me toward a place of resting.

Even if this *or* that, *you're accepted and loved*, he tells me. *Nothing, and I mean* nothing, *baby girl, has the power to remove you from my best for you.*

I'm loved and have what I need to make it through.

God tells my mind and heart, *I'll see you through this change, Kristen. Keep your eyes on the facts of your faith, not your feelings of fear.*

Christ's love compels me toward a place of resting.

So I pivot from the brownies (a good idea on several fronts) and read about how Jesus came to give us life and give it abundantly.[2] I read afresh David's words in Psalm 23:

> Even though I walk through the valley of the shadow of death,
> I will fear no evil,
> for you are with me;
> your rod and your staff,
> they comfort me. (v. 4)

David says that even though he walks through scary times, he walks with the Lord, and the Lord's promises stand as a protective barrier between him and the fear. The fear, even fear brought on by evil intent, doesn't have God's permission to enter. In the words of Oswald Chambers,

> We are "more than conquerors in all these things." Paul is not talking of imaginary things, but of things that are desperately actual; and he says we are super-victors in the midst of them, not by our ingenuity, or by our courage, or by anything other than the fact that not one of them affects our relationship to God in Jesus Christ.[3]

Once again, I sit my hind end in my chair to get back to writing. I acknowledge the fears at the table, but they don't take over things. Regardless of how I feel, *I am a super-victor*.

I look up to see a brushstroke of fuchsia over Pikes Peak tonight, like a ribbon of hope curling 'round that towering mountain.

Like a ribbon of hope that refuses to fade, the kind of hope that circles and covers a mountain of fear.

May you and I keep moving through our change and everything it brings, not because we have no fear but because in the smallest of ways we're brave enough to live from how the Creator made us and out of Jesus's love for us.

And may our faith, rather than our fears, determine where we go and what we do next.

Dear Father, you're completely aware of the fear that circles my heart before landing with a thud in my stomach. However, I know your Word says that your perfect love casts out fear. I know your Word says you have not given us a spirit of fear but of love, power, and a sound mind. Please infuse in me an awareness that if fear isn't from you, it has no hold on me, and I can fulfill the assignment you've made for my life. Please flood me with your love. Please remind me that the same power that raised Jesus from the dead is available to raise up a holy confidence within me. Quiet down my mind when it races to all the what-if places and send it and my heart to your embrace. In the loving name of Jesus, amen.

"Don't speak to it as is. Speak to it as it will be when it reaches the hands of Jesus Christ." ~Priscilla Shirer

Fear does not have God's permission to enter you.
Let faith and not fears be the focus of your thoughts and actions during change. Live out of how the Creator made you and out of Jesus's love for you, not out of fear.

DAY 5

First, Go

For what does the Scripture say? "Abraham believed God, and it was accounted to him for righteousness."
Romans 4:3 NKJV

I walked out to our porch for the hundredth time, thinking just maybe I'd catch a glimpse of my son James, who at that moment was sitting in the pilot's seat of a small private airplane up among the clouds. Since that plane was nowhere near our house, I couldn't. Still, I looked skyward just the same, comforted by the fact that it was as Colorado blue as could be. "Well, he couldn't ask for better flying weather," I said out loud to myself.

For the past several months, James had been taking flying lessons with the goal of getting his private pilot's license. His flight instructor, a kindly older fellow named Hank, usually sat in the cockpit with James, but this time James sat alone. On this particular spring day, James was flying his first "cross country solo flight." That meant he'd fly over a southeastern swath of Colorado's brown earth, landing and taking off again from a handful of small airports.

Of course, I couldn't use any twenty-first-century "find my phone" app to track him in the sky. However, my husband, David, had an air band radio, which is a handy-dandy tool that picks up airplane radio frequencies. I knew what time James should be returning to his home base of Meadow Lake Airport, so I tuned the air band radio to that airport's frequency. Once I heard his voice on that radio, my mama-heart could relax and let me get on with the rest of my day.

When the time came for him to arrive, I turned on the radio and started to listen. And listen. *And listen.* And while I heard a lot of pilot chatter, I didn't hear James. For forty-five minutes, I fought the panic monsters as they tried to drag me toward the intersection of Anxiety Drive and Worst-Case Scenario. But eventually, I started to travel that direction anyway. I paced back and forth on our side porch, my mind racing with all that could've gone wrong. I looked up at the sky. I looked down at the radio in my hands. No matter how I pleaded, I couldn't will my child's voice to materialize.

Finally, after one whole hour that crawled along glacier-forming slow, I heard James make his "final approach" call as well as his response after landing. I sunk down into one of our rocking chairs and let out one of the biggest sighs of my life.

In hindsight, I know this all sounds rather melodramatic, but I don't care. I was just so relieved he was okay.

When James returned home, his excitement level was in the clouds, and he practically levitated as he told me how amazing it was to fly solo. I wanted to respond with a plea that while this was all fabulous, he needed to stay on the ground like a sensible person from here on out. Instead, I offered him my excitement and support. Because that's what we moms often have to do: back our children up when we'd rather scream, "FOR THE LOVE OF ALL THAT'S HOLY PLEASE JUST STAY PUT AND DON'T GET YOURSELF KILLED."

Change comes in so many shades and silhouettes. When my husband was on active duty, it largely came by way of moving around and all the starting over that came with that. These days, our changing locations are more metaphorical, like parenting nearly grown children. It's still new territory, and I struggle to settle myself into a place where I can see the blessings it brings.

I wonder if Abram (who later became Abraham) had the same thought when the Lord said to him,

> Get out of your country,
> From your family
> And from your father's house,
> To a land that I will show you.
> I will make you a great nation;
> I will bless you
> And make your name great;
> And you shall be a blessing. . . .
> And in you all the families of the earth shall be blessed.
> (Gen. 12:1–3 NKJV)

In verse 4, we learn that Abram left as the Lord had told him to. In obedience, Abram went where God directed because he took God at his word and trusted the blessings to follow. Whether you know transition under your feet, in your heart, or both, the Lord is bringing you someplace new for the purpose of blessing you. In the words of John Piper, Abraham was not a cul-de-sac of that blessing but a conduit to the rest of us.[1] The promise God spoke to Abraham is the same offered to you and me.

If God's promise to Abraham—and to the rest of us—brings about blessings, we then know change is a provision of God's grace.

Whether you know transition under your feet, in your heart, or both, the Lord is bringing you someplace new for the purpose of blessing you.

Whatever change is in your life and scaring the daggum daylights out of you, know that it is okay to shed tears over it. It's okay to feel overwhelmed by it. Acknowledge those feelings to God and know he understands. Remember too that Jesus felt weakness, and he isn't put out by our weakness. As you acknowledge the real losses this change brings, also acknowledge that, like Jesus's resurrection on Easter morning, this difficult change will not be the end of everything but the birthing of a new beginning.

May we, like Abraham, obey and trust the blessings to follow.

Almighty God, you know how scared—even terrified—I am about this change you're asking me to walk through. Help me lay out on the table every troubling thought I have with it. Help me acknowledge how hard it is for me to let you take the wheel (and the wheel of my loved ones' lives). Will you show me how, in the middle of its crazy, I can still rest in you? I trust and believe you, Lord, that you're using this change to change me for the better—that this change is a grace. Help me live this truth out on the outside by calming me down on the inside. In the saving name of Jesus, amen.

"You may need to let go of that deluded belief that if you worry about something enough, it will resolve itself. . . . Worry changes nothing. Trust changes everything."
~Jennifer Dukes Lee, It's All Under Control

God's promise to Abraham is the same promise for you: the Lord has brought this change to you for the purpose of blessing you. Obey him and trust the blessings to follow.

DAY 6

Look for the Signs

Oh, how abundant is your goodness, which you have stored up for those who fear you and worked for those who take refuge in you.

Psalm 31:19

It was our sons' last day of Christmas vacation, and our family of five was spending it in the mountain towns of Keystone and nearby Dillon, Colorado. The drive to Keystone should only take two and a half hours, but three accidents and a white-out snowstorm along I-70 dictated otherwise. After no small amount of travel drama, we finally made it into town, parked our cars, and put on ski pants, jackets, and all the paraphernalia before tubing—our activity *du jour*. Following check-in, we stood in line amid many snowboard- and ski-carrying folks to ride the gondola to the top of the mountain.

After the fifteen-minute ride, we hopped out and made our way to the little round hut where an attendant relayed our tubing information. After signing waivers and watching a safety video, we found our tubes and got in line for one of the six tubing runs. My husband and I decided to go together, reasoning our combined weight would help us glide faster down the hill. (Read: we're a little competitive and wanted to beat the kids to the bottom.) When it was our turn to go, a resort employee dressed in a dozen layers gave us a good shove, and away we went. We flew faster than I thought we would, and for a moment or two I was airborne. I landed and we continued to sail along, me laughing so hard I could barely breathe. The arctic air snatched what breath I did have, and the flying bits of ice and snow made it hard to open my eyes. We arrived at the bottom of the hill, and my stomach hurt for laughing so hard. For the next hour, we got in half a dozen more tubing runs. I took some videos and pictures, but mostly I took armloads of good memories of our family together, worth far more than the price of admission.

After tubing, we visited the famed ice castles in Dillon, where the *Frozen* soundtrack skated all around us. My daughter astutely pointed out that the area was more "ice walls" than ice castles—it's a little bit of a letdown. While visiting here was a good part of a great day together, we're not so sure this place was worth the price of admission.

At this point, the sun hovered quietly over the western Rockies and our stomachs rumbled with hunger. We made our way to a local brewery, where we enjoyed conversation and a few rounds of Hangman with our burgers and fries. But all too soon, it was time for David, Faith, and I to hug our beloved boys' necks and tell them goodbye. After sharing the interstate with us for a while in the car behind us, they'd head north toward school and we'd head south toward home. It had been one glorious month of having them with us, and Faith and I cried because we didn't want it to end.

As we wound our way through the steep-grade roads toward Denver, I thought about how change can be so much like this family day. Depending on your own circumstances, it can be worth the price of admission, especially if it's a welcome change. But often change doesn't feel like it's worth it, at least not for a while. The cost is just too high, and you might be awfully tired of crying your eyes out over it. You're very annoyed and disappointed that time hasn't healed the sadness that came with the change.

We reached Denver, and James and Ethan turned to take I-25 north while we exited onto I-25 south. Though I know that my boys were traveling the direction they're supposed to, it was painful to know it was the opposite direction of my own.

Time doesn't heal all wounds; rather, time with the Healer does.

Change can make your heart travel in opposite directions.

I'm sad, and I'm tired of time taking its time in making this whole transition easier. But this I hold on to: time doesn't heal all wounds; rather, time with the Healer does.

So, that day I talked silently to the Lord about my frustrations. As the shadows gave way to darkness outside my car window, I sensed the smallest lightening inside me.

I will see the goodness of the Lord in the land of the living.[1]

And with that, I knew he meant for me to receive this message: *Just hang on. Keep spending time with me, and you'll see all the ways I'll redeem this time.*

Even as I repeatedly acknowledge the loss and sadness brought on by change, it's well and good to acknowledge his goodness in store for me before I know its details. I sense that, in some way, any hardship he brings through this change—any change—will be worth the price of admission.

Sure, I may sometimes wish the change never came my way, but I also hold on to the fact that the hardship it brings matters. God makes it all matter.

We arrived home, and Faith and I walked inside and acknowledged that the house felt different without our boys thumping around like German shepherds. Late in the evening, I sat in my office chair and opened my laptop to write a few words. And that's when I found a white sticky note on my keyboard. Written in one son's angular handwriting, it said a simple but satisfying "Miss you!"

And I teared up again, in the good way, thankful that while this change is so difficult, it comes with blessed signs of love, care, and attention.

I believe more are to come.

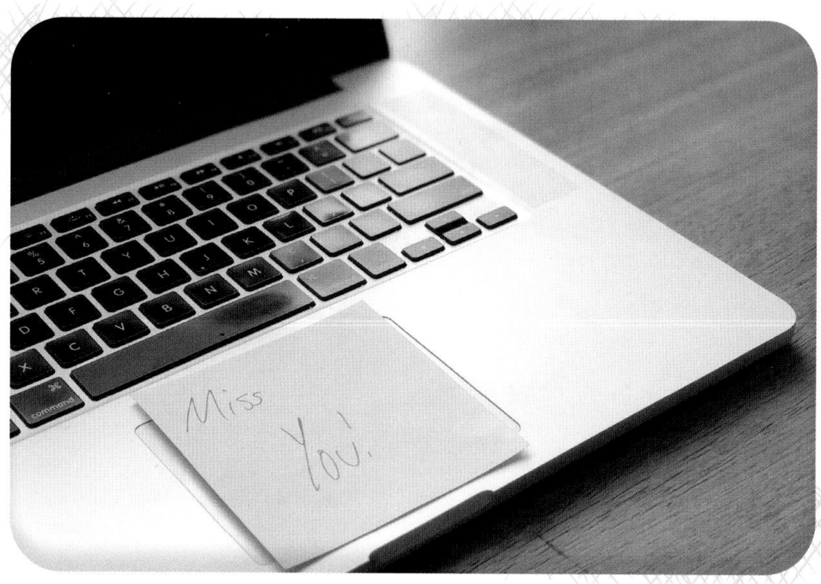

God, thank you for seeing me through this transition moment by moment, hour by hour, day by day. As you promise in Psalm 68, continue to bear me up through your very real presence. Like a cheerful hidden note sparks joy when found, send an outside message to me so I know on the inside that you see me and are working in my circumstances and life. Thank you for your Son, Jesus, who spared nothing for me so I could have everything in him. In his kind, compassionate name, amen.

"Jesus may ask of you far more than you planned to give, but He can give to you infinitely more than you dared ask or think."
~Tim Keller, King's Cross

The hardships your change brings matter, and you can acknowledge the good to come before you see it. Time doesn't heal all wounds change brings. Time with the Healer does.

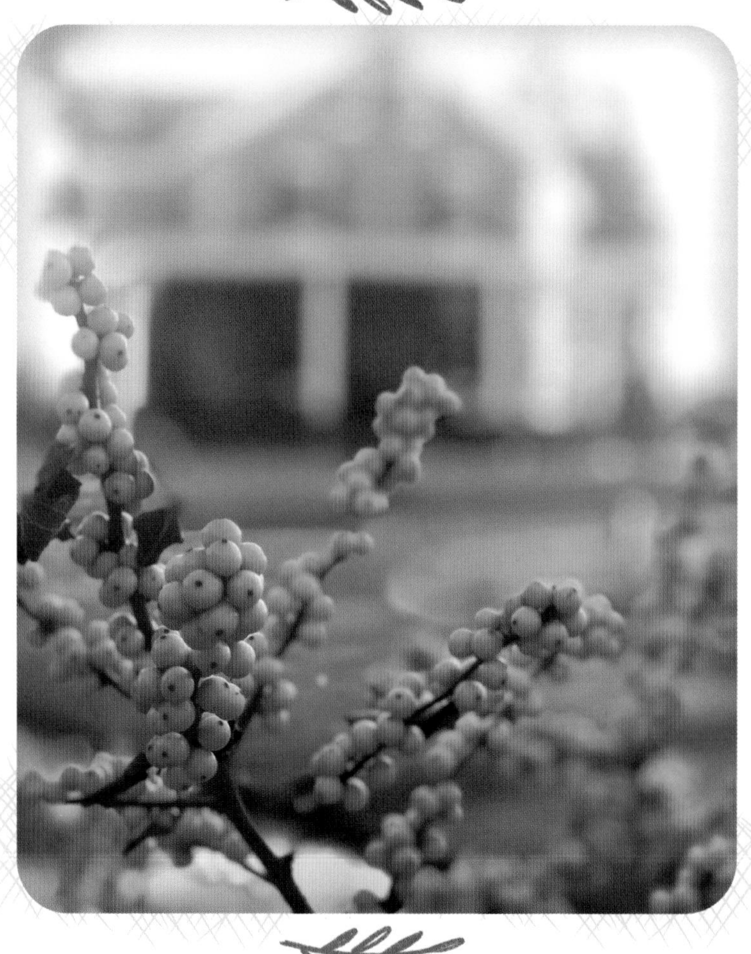

DAY 7

Grow Good Things

Behold, the former things have come to pass, and new things I now declare; before they spring forth I tell you of them.

Isaiah 42:9

For the entire flight from Dallas, Texas, to Charlotte, North Carolina, I wrangled my twin three-year-old sons in their seats on either side of me. Six months pregnant with my daughter, Faith, this was no easy task. The sole adult accompanying my two (and a half) wee-watts, I looked forward to arriving at our friends' beautiful home in Asheville at their invitation. We lived in Albuquerque at the time, and my husband frequently traveled for work. So, a springtime trip to the lush, green South after a very brown winter was my kind of welcome change—and worth wrangling small children on a couple of plane rides.

Finally, our plane began its descent over Charlotte, and James and Ethan became positively enamored with what they saw outside. James, eyes wide as jumbo pancakes, looked out from his window seat and shouted, "Wow, Mama! Look at all those trees! I've never seen so many trees!" Meanwhile, Ethan, sitting on the other side of me, strained over my lap to get a look alongside his brother. He squealed and tapped my leg ninety to nothing, exclaiming, "And water! Mama! James! Look at all that water! I can't believe there's so much water!"

My tiny children, who'd lived in the Midwest before moving to the sparsely treed desert, acted like this was the literal first time they'd ever seen water and trees. I looked around and smiled at the other passengers staring at us, hoping they didn't assume I'd had these children locked up in a closet till now.

Seeing those things in such bountiful supply positively mesmerized my kids. It brought a brand-new kind of beauty to them that they enjoyed to the hilt—as did their mama.

Last December, I enjoyed the placemaking beauty of my friend Christie in Pennsylvania. She lives in a house older than a century or two, and some of the trees around her farmhouse are even older. I marveled at the harvest-orange winterberries standing sentinel at the end of her driveway, simply gobsmacked that such beauty on fire could rage on in the cold of December.

Today, I live in the high desert town of Colorado Springs, where we get more moisture than Albuquerque (read: powdery snow) but get cooler temperatures too. This translates to a short growing season that really tests my greenish thumb. I want to be able to haphazardly throw seeds and small plants into the ground like I imagine Christie can in Pennsylvania, or North Carolinians do in their neck of the woods. But the truth is that for every plant I successfully coax above ground here in Colorado, I've got two or three more that didn't make it. Even if I managed to water and fertilize the plants as directed, grasshoppers, deer, late spring frosts, or unforgiving summer hailstorms may take them out.

To experience a region's particular kind of beauty, you must also experience the loss. In Albuquerque, folks enjoy the most spectacular desert sunsets, but they experience a loss of vegetation. In Colorado, we have a long ski season and lots of sunshine, but the arid climate makes it harder to grow things. North Carolinians and Pennsylvanians enjoy an abundance of lush vegetation, but at the expense of as many sunshine-filled days. Every single gift or strength comes with a shadow, and sometimes it comes down to your preferences as to which is which.

Whether you live in New Mexico or Colorado or Pennsylvania or North Carolina, you can't grow a single thing without some kind of loss. You can't grow a single thing without a big change from the very beginning—you lose the seed as it breaks open and changes into the plant or flower or tree.

It's been a season where change has made me break open too, and I feel the pains of growing. In the midst of my own painful change, I struggle with the verses in Romans that tell us to rejoice in suffering. *Who in their right mind gets excited over pain?* I think to myself. But then I read it again:

> Not only that, but we rejoice in our sufferings, knowing that suffering produces endurance, and endurance produces character, and character produces hope. (Rom. 5:3–4)

Suffering is the seed breaking, turning into shoots of endurance. Endurance looks like shoots becoming sturdy trees, growing in width of character. Finally, the trees grow in height of maturity and hope, producing a canopy of shelter and protection that wouldn't be there without the suffering in the first place.

Abundance and scarcity are sisters, both bringing the possibility of thriving, even when it looks different from the way I think it's supposed to look. I can rejoice in the suffering change brings when I see what it leads to: growth that brings good things I couldn't otherwise fathom. Growth that makes me stronger, grittier, and better able to endure the potholed roads of life. Growth that leads me to a place of maturity and hope.

The change is not a waste.

Depending on the elements, getting through difficult change—and growing through it—can take a little effort or a whole lot of it. But take heart, dear one. The hard work is not a waste. The change is not a waste. What's lost isn't a waste. It will lead somewhere meaningful—to a canopy covering a bright future full of new mercies and meaningful growth in a stronger, sturdier you.

Dear Father God, I thank you that while I'm standing in the middle of so much loss, you've allowed this change because you already see how it's growing and maturing me. You see it leading to a more hopeful future for me. Before my pulse quickens because of all the unknowns, please calm my anxious heart. Before I start to panic, give me your peace that passes all understanding; give me your knowledge that my suffering will not be the end. Thank you that because of your redemptive heart, loss leads to growing good things in abundance. Thank you for your Son, Jesus, who went the ultimate distance so I could know ultimate love. In his mighty name, amen.

"Like winter, the wilderness is always a promise. God leads us in and, one way or another, he leads us out again."
~Christie Purifoy, Placemaker

Change—and its losses—helps you grow toward a more hopeful future.

GOD'S PROMISES ARE BELIEVABLE,
AND HIS PRESENCE IS UNCHANGEABLE.

DAY 8

Remember the Relationship

Every valley shall be lifted up, and every mountain and hill be made low; the uneven ground shall become level, and the rough places a plain. . . . For the mouth of the LORD has spoken.

Isaiah 40:4–5

On the National Geographic program *Running Wild*, host Bear Grylls, a former member of the British Special Forces and all-around survival instructor, takes celebrities (even one former US president) to remote locations around the globe for "an adventure of a lifetime." We viewers are eyewitnesses to these adventures as we watch Bear and his A-list guests eat everything from cockroaches to maggots. (They're high in protein, after all!) We watch them, among other things, climb mountains with only a flimsy rope ladder and their upper body strength. We watch Bear pep-talk his co-adventurers into crossing deep canyons and catching a fish (aka dinner) with their bare hands. One thing is for sure: Bear pushes his guests' bodies and minds to their limits.

As you might imagine, some celebrities handle this better than others. On *Running Wild*'s predecessor show, *Man vs. Wild*, actor Jake Gyllenhaal showed such courage on his Icelandic adventure that when a blizzard set in, he took the lead across snowy terrain chock-full of hidden crevasses and stayed calm in spite of falling into one.[1] On the other hand, when one of our favorite *Friends*, Courteney Cox, rappelled down a sheer cliff in Ireland with the churning sea below, she full-on panicked, crying and dropping enough F-bombs to impress Leonardo DiCaprio.[2]

What it comes down to, it seems, is how much Bear's guests trust him to get them through each challenge. Those who lean into what he asks them to do—and don't spend all their time questioning and second-guessing his directions—are those who rappel the cliff or climb the mountain or eat the fish eyeballs (!!!) with less struggle and more conserved energy. A change in procedure could always happen, but Bear always has a plan B. At some point, each person has to trust that Bear and his team have their best interest at heart and know how to keep them safe. At some point, they have to lean into the fact that Bear and his team have gone ahead and scouted the route. Bear knows how to get each person from the beginning of the adventure to their extraction point down the road (or up to the mountain summit). And every single celebrity guest is thrilled to reach that extraction point—their entry place to celebrating that *indeed, they made it.*

And so it goes with the change in our lives: Do we trust that God has gone ahead, knows every detail of the route we'll walk through, and will one way or another see us through it?

Do we lean into him or panic, cry, and cuss? Maybe both?

As I hope I've already made clear, it isn't wrong to lament the change—whatever that looks like for you. It isn't wrong to feel whatever you honestly feel. It certainly isn't wrong to ask God questions—the Bible is full of folks who laid them on him. But when the dust settles and the shock subsides, we can cling to the rock-solid promise that our Guide will get us through.

We can cling to the Guide's book, where we're guided toward all manner of assurances for our life change. In God's Word, I'm reminded that the Lord helps see us through change in all kinds of ordinary and extraordinary ways. As he delivered David from Saul, the Lord enables us to leap over walls.[3] The Lord makes nothing of soaring hills and bottomless basins.[4] Someway, somehow, he'll straighten your path and my path and give us the ability to traverse it.

Change surely brings us to untamed, off-the-grid territory. But when we stay connected to God through his Word, we study and learn that he can be trusted to always have our best interests at heart. We're in a much better position to make it through whatever lies ahead. We're more apt to accept the change God allows. It may be new territory for us, but it's old hat for him.

Ruth Chou Simons says this about consistency in the Word:

> Relationship will always be a greater motivator than ritual. If you're looking to be more consistent in your Bible this year, remind yourself that God's Word is a love letter and a hearty meal at your Father's table.[5]

Remember the relationship, and your training for this running wild kind of life will follow suit.

Bear, who has a real affable and gentle nature, often gets folks to open up and share personal details in ways not often seen in typical media interviews. And sometimes I wonder if that's the real purpose of the journey. Not to simply experience an epic adventure, but to reap the rewards of a meaningful connection.

When I'm breathing in the Word, I'm breathing out a better day.

Likewise, read God's Word for the connection—and connect yourself to the Guide during all circumstances.

At the end of the day, this is one thing I've found to be true: when I'm breathing in the Word, I'm breathing out a better day.

When you and I are breathing in the Word, we're breathing out regular reminders that God will get us through this day, this season, and this change.

And it will lead to our own time of celebrating that *indeed, we made it*.

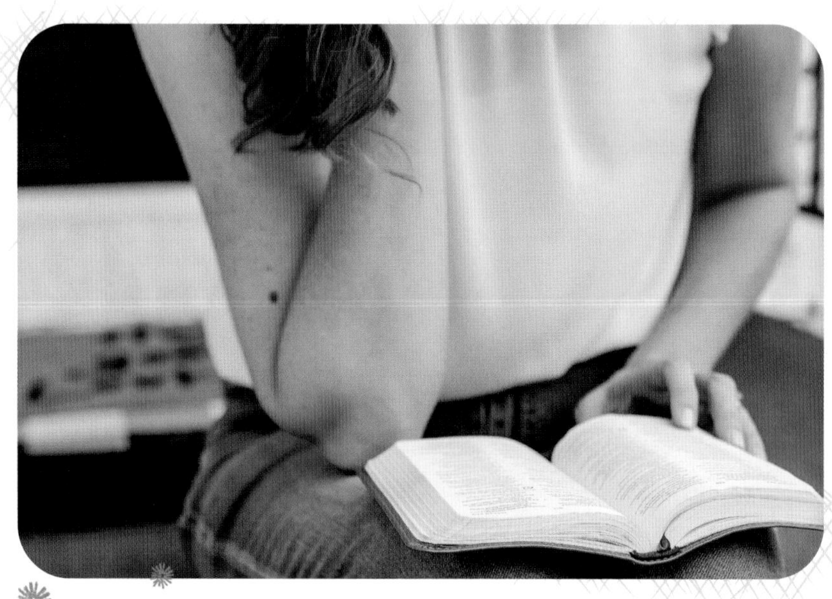

Dear Father in heaven, I know that if you're asking me to walk through some scary places in this change, it's only because where I'm going will have me in a better place than where I am now. You know how terrified I feel over the unfamiliar. Help me remember that I won't always feel this way. Grow in me a desire to consistently read your Word so I can see this change from a truthful, hopeful perspective. I ask all these things in the loving name of your Son, Jesus. Amen.

"The message of the Bible is not about God in Heaven who wants to take from you. It's about God who wants to give to you." ~Francis Chan

Feed your relationship with God through reading his Word—and be regularly reminded that your Guide will usher you through this change.

DAY 9

Talking Back to Your Strong-Willed Self

You hem me in, behind and before, and lay your hand upon me.

Psalm 139:5

When we lived in Albuquerque, New Mexico, I spent most every noon hour on summer weekdays at Pershing Park with my precious young'uns. At that time (and I believe still today), the city generously offered free picnic lunches at various locations citywide for children ages one to eighteen. Alongside several of my neighborhood mom-friends and their kids, my three young children enjoyed simple lunches of peanut butter or ham sandwiches and applesauce with a bag of chips or a chocolate chip cookie. I tell ya, for the three summers we lived in that desert town, kids and parents alike relished "picnic at the park" lunch dates. Our children could eat a suitable lunch and see their friends while we parents enjoyed a few blessed minutes of conversation while the kids played.

On that front, my standard rule for where my kids could play included the expansive grassy area where we ate as well as the playground equipment located on one end. Three fairly busy streets hemmed in this park, so my kids weren't allowed to go on the sidewalk that surrounded the grassy area. If they stayed off the sidewalk, I knew they'd stay a healthy distance from the traffic on the roads beyond it.

While all three kids tested that limit from time to time, one of my precious darlings full-on resented the limitation. Deliberate as the day is long, he would repeatedly inch toward the sidewalk while keeping his eyes laser-focused on me. Then, he would walk the line that divided the grass and sidewalk just to see what I would do, daring me to call him out.

Great day, this beloved offspring of mine could be so strong-willed, he'd reduce a drill sergeant to tears. He reduced *this* mama to tears, that's for sure. I plumb wore myself out holding him accountable for his choices.

As exhausting as parenting this child was in the little years, I have to own up to the fact that he takes after me in more ways than one. Certainly, my own strong-willed streak has been known to rise up from a change I didn't ask for or want. But more specifically, I balk at limitations that the change brings. I want to do what I want and go where I want without some kind of overreaching entity or parent telling me *no*.

I'm forty-six and still don't like to hear the word *no* when what I want to hear is *yes*. I blame my own personality limitation that says, "Change just doesn't come easily for me, so of course I can't thrive within these limitations!" I maintain a resentful side-eye to change rather than work to accept it.

But when I *do* work to accept it, I see that God wants to use those limitations for me rather than against me.

Life's limitations are God's invitation to change my expectations. Limitations unfold God's intentions for me to travel a narrower path of possibilities.

If I'm still being honest with myself, I admit that having an endless menu of options free of restrictions is overwhelming and can slow me down. There's a freedom that comes with limitations—a freedom in finite choices. If something isn't available to me because the change took it away, then I don't need to devote time to obsessing over it. I can tell my pride—and my pile of expectations hitched to it—to have a seat and simply wait and see what valuable gifts God might bring my way through the limitations, not in spite of them.

While the good life isn't free of limitations, God gives limitless attention to our best—his *all*s and *no*s are always for my good.

> For the word of the Lord is upright, and *all* his work is done in faithfulness. (Ps. 33:4, emphasis mine)

> The young lions suffer want and hunger; but those who seek the Lord lack *no* good thing. (34:10, emphasis mine)

> The Lord is good to *all*, and his mercy is over *all* that he has made. (145:9, emphasis mine)

We may not have any idea what will come calling in our future, but we have God's faithful *all* and *no* working on our behalf and in our corner always. Life's limitations are still all for us—and can take no good thing from us.

Today, that strong-willed child o' mine is a delightful young adult who's a natural servant-leader and encourager of others. That can be the reward of strong-willed kids: adults who lead and love well. (It's just heck on us parents getting them there!) As a little one, he didn't have the ability to take the long view of the good found in limitations. But now he does. He sees the wisdom in the limitations we gave him—at least usually. (Grin.)

Life's limitations are still all for us—and can take no good thing from us.

I'm working on seeing the wisdom in God's limitations too.

My counselor, Gwen, told me about a study that looked at how children behaved on school playgrounds with fences around them and how they behaved on playgrounds without fences. The study found that on those school playgrounds without fences, the children didn't stray too far from their teacher. However, on the school playgrounds with fences, the kids ran all over the place, exploring every inch the playground had to offer.

Limitations, like boundaries, give freedom and help our relationships for the long haul. Limitations show love and feed our sense of belonging.

Limitations help us accept change—by acting as borders that hem us in and keep us on the path God prepares for us. Limitations are tools God uses to help us learn to serve, lead, and love others well.

I don't want to say *no* to all God has for me because I say *no* to the limitations he gives me.

May you and I keep our hearts open to accept what we can't see or know right now. One day we *will* see it: our gratitude for the limitations we didn't think we wanted but can now know we needed.

Dear Father, you know I still get mad about this change I didn't ask for or want. I don't want to be like an obstinate preschooler, but it's so hard to accept how these limitations have changed my plans. Give me a new thing to hope for, a vision of your all in mind for me and my loved ones. Help me to remain receptive and not resentful of life's limitations. Help me to remember that when you add a limitation to my life, it's to help me change my expectations. Thank you that you love me no matter how fine the line I walk between trusting you and wanting to be my own boss. In the name of Jesus, amen.

"Trust God's no." ~Beth Moore

Life's limitations are God's invitation to change my expectations. His limitations are all for me and can take no good thing from me.

DAY 10

When All You See Are Bugs, Look Again

Rejoice always, pray continually, give thanks in all circumstances; for this is God's will for you in Christ Jesus.

1 Thessalonians 5:16–18 NIV

Kick your feet up and relax while I describe one picturesque, breathtaking place our family lived. Endless scenic beaches, amazing views, stunning sunsets—it had it all. The temperature was a perfect 85 degrees nearly every day of the year. Those miles of flawless beaches hemmed in a stunning interior that quite possibly resembled the Garden of Eden.

We enjoyed all the ocean and mountains had to offer at any season. We spent every momentous occasion from Jesus's birthday to our kids' birthdays playing in the sand, and we passed the days of winter watching whales leap and frolic in the ocean. Life tasted sweet and ripe, like a sticky, mouth-watering mango. We sauntered through life there with a relaxed heart rate while stillness became our friend.

Now, lean in and listen as I describe a much less ideal place we lived. Locals were sometimes closed off to outsiders, and even my kids acutely felt this at their neighborhood school. More than once I had someone hand me harsh, unsolicited parenting advice for the smallest of "infractions." Our living expenses were out of this world, and our swollen monthly rent check was only outdone by our monthly grocery bill. I still shudder when I think about how, while checking out at the grocery store one day, I watched a single cantaloupe ring up at $10. Instantly, I jerked up my hand and said, "Wait! I don't need cantaloupe that badly!"

This same place with the pricey fruit had mild year-round weather, but no cold season meant the flying cockroaches and scurrying centipedes were big enough to carry away small children. Its staple export required field burning before harvesting, so often the air was thick with a sickening smell. And burning fields weren't the only stench invading the air. With an active volcano located on a neighboring island, the foggy substance *vog*—smoglike volcanic air pollution that contains sulfur dioxide—routinely hung low in the air, limiting our pretty views. These were things you might miss on a vacation, but living there meant they smacked you upside the head on as many days as they didn't.

Now, I'm sure you're onto me here, but I'll just say it anyway: *both places I described are really the exact same place.*

Same place, different perspectives.

Similarly, it's a change in perspective that makes all the difference in accepting a difficult change in our lives, and there's nothing that helps us change our perspective faster than practicing gratitude.

Perhaps Ann Voskamp says it best in *The Greatest Gift*:

> Joy is a function of gratitude, and gratitude is a function of perspective. You only begin to change your life when you begin to change the way you see.[1]

Practicing gratitude doesn't mean we're suddenly blind to the hardships of our change. We don't "transcend" their presence or act like they're not there. And we don't refuse to look them in the eye. Rather, it means that after we look our challenges in the eye and acknowledge their presence, we shift our focus to feast on what we're thankful for so we can begin to *accept* their presence.

I'm often in awe of Paul's gratitude sprinkled throughout the New Testament as he faced a truckload of difficulties. In several of his letters, he gives heartfelt thanks for those folks receiving his letters. And when Paul is stuck at sea during a violent storm, he still gives thanks for the blessings right in front of him. Was he also retching over the side of the boat? Did he worry he'd be swimming at sea for hours? I have no idea, but this is what we do know:

> After [Paul] said this, he took some bread and gave thanks to God in front of them all. Then he broke it and began to eat. They were all encouraged and ate some food themselves. (Acts 27:35–36 NIV)

Paul gave thanks to God.

He and his shipmates ate bread.

They were all encouraged.

When we give thanks and feast on what is right in front of us, we are encouraged. Gratitude is a lifeline to hold on to when change takes away what we hold dear. Gratitude is an open window in the stifling room of anxiety and dread. Open the window of gratitude and feel the cool breeze and warm light as it refreshes and revives you into focusing on what you have rather than what you don't.

When we give thanks, we feel different on the inside so we can live differently on the outside.

Paul's example proves that even as stormy circumstances attack on all fronts, we'll still be encouraged through gratitude. When we give thanks, we're rewarded—with a shift in perspective and a shot of encouragement.

When we give thanks, we feel different on the inside so we can live differently on the outside.

Not long ago, I felt the Lord imprint a strong message of gratitude on my heart. He asked me to think of Matthew 25:23 in a new light.

> You have been faithful with a few things; I will put you in charge of many things. (NIV)

The Lord used this verse to ask me a question: *Kristen, if you will not be thankful for a few things, why should I give you many things?*

Why indeed.

When change hits us hard, may gratitude rather than grumbling be our long-view default. May we actively resolve to be quietly involved in seeking out God's rainstorm of daily blessings. And may we actively resolve to offer up gratitude in all things—showing God we trust him to use all things.

Dear Father God, I thank and praise you for all your generous provision. I'm so sorry for all the times I turn my nose up to your gifts and choose grumbling over gratitude. This change raises up in me such fears, but I know you will quell those fears when I name the gifts you give me right now. Open my eyes to the beauty around me, and may you cultivate in me a heart that sees your hand in everything. I love you, and I am eternally thankful for your Son, Jesus. In his name I pray, amen.

"'We're all blessed and we're all blighted, Chief Inspector,' said Finney. 'Every day each of us does our sums. The question is, what do we count?'" ~Louise Penny, A Rule Against Murder

See, name, and give thanks to God for what he gives and receive an encouraging shift in perspective that helps you accept the change in your life. Be thankful for a few things and receive many things.

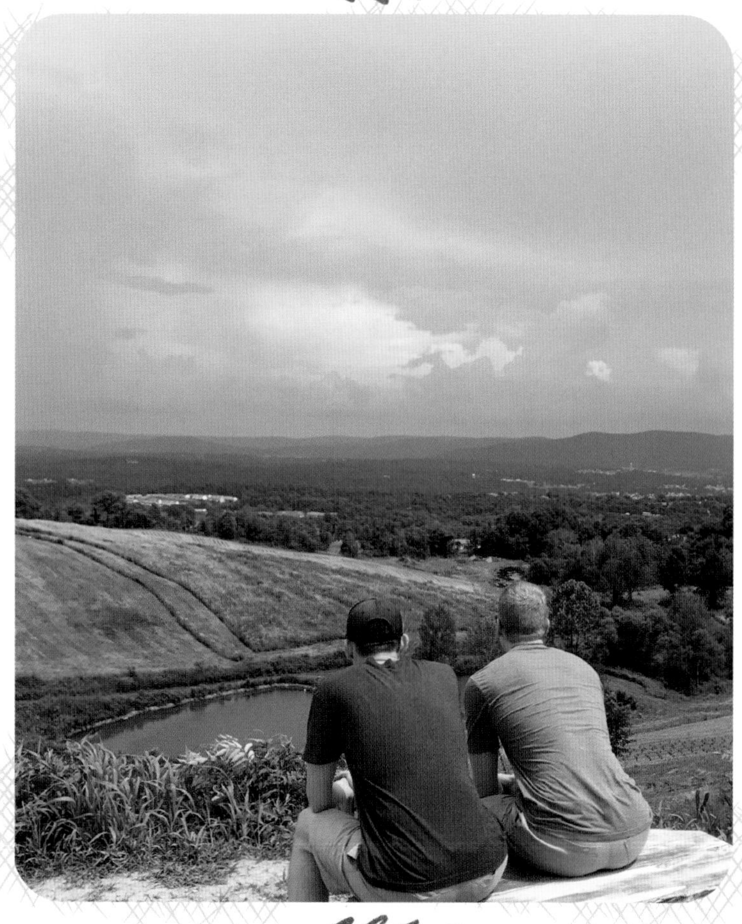

DAY 11

Sit and Support

Tell the next generation detail by detail the story of God.

Psalm 48:13 Message

A while ago, I read a quote by former first lady Michelle Obama that went like this: "When people ask me how I'm doing . . . I say, 'I'm only as good as my most sad child.'"[1] I thought, *Well, Michelle, I hear ya there.* I'll take a hundred dreadful changes that impact only me over a single one that affects a loved one, in particular one of my kiddos. Few things stir up my anxious feelings more than watching a child or other loved one go through painful troubles.

What I wouldn't do to take the suffering away—to absorb it myself so he or she didn't have to carry it at all.

That's what I was thinking recently as I slowed my car into the drop-off circle in front of my daughter's high school. Faith was going through a humdinger of a season due to several difficult changes, and my heart felt especially heavy as I came to a stop. As is my habit, before she got out of the car, I strove to make like Coach Monica from *Cheer* and offer her a meaningful pep talk. I did my best to build her up before who-knows-what worked to break her down during the day.

I told her, "Faith, you're a beloved child of God, full of integrity and strength and a dozen other gifts and talents. You're loved beyond reason by Jesus, your family, and so many others. Walk in the confidence of who you are today, baby girl."

Faith gave me a weak smile and said, "I love you, Mama." Then she left the car. I barely got out of the parking lot before my heavy heart began leaking out of my eyeballs.

We dads and mamas pray for our kids to learn perseverance, humility, compassion, and a closeness and dependency on the Lord. But then we forget these things are acquired through difficulties that leave their hearts—and ours—flattened like roadkill on pavement. We forget those character qualities are forged through fire because all we can think about is how we'd dearly love to shield our babies from the heat. But to do so would be to shield them from the important formation that comes with—and from—the loss and heartache.

As Mary witnessed her son, Jesus, suffer on the cross beyond all comprehension, I imagine she would've moved heaven and earth to rescue him. When Jesus told her that John would be her son and she his mother, I wonder if she thought to herself, *But* you're *the son I need and want, dear boy.* At the time, did she have any inkling her son had to walk through excruciating change so her own future—and indeed, all our futures—could be changed for the better?

Mary losing her child saved us all—and gave us all his enduring presence. And out of that presence, Jesus tells us

I am with you through this, dear one.[2]

Let's get away to a quiet corner and enjoy a little rest.[3]

Encountering difficulties is a sure thing, beloved, but my conquering them is the surest thing.[4]

More often than not, we can't fix or manage the difficulties our loved ones endure. We can't talk them into our way of thinking. And that's a good thing, because if we could do any of those things, our loved ones would be less likely to see their need for Jesus. There can be only one Savior, and sometimes we must trust the work he's doing is helping others from the inside out.

There can be only one Savior, and sometimes we must trust the work he's doing is helping others from the inside out.

However, what we *can* do is model Jesus's presence next to them and his words of affirmation for them.

> For we do not have a high priest who is unable to sympathize with our weaknesses, but one who in every respect has been tempted as we are, yet without sin. Let us then with confidence draw near to the throne of grace, that we may receive mercy and find grace to help in time of need. (Heb. 4:15–16)

Jesus knows what it's like to be us and how hard it is to handle deep struggles and graduate school–level problems. He gives us a place to set those struggles—his lap—and prayer as the way we can do so.

So, here's to praying for our loved ones and letting the Rescuer tend to them.

Here's to accepting that pain is one thing that opens our eyes to the many ways God is faithful, present, and compassionate—and an arrow that points our loved ones to those things.

And here's to being a safe place for our loved ones as they sift through and process their change.

I have friends with adult children who tell me the ache and sadness over changes that affect children never leave a parent's heart. You just get more practiced at accepting the needed work and lessons it brings with it.

No life worth living is free and easy, but Jesus paid it all so we could have all hope within our reach.

He paid it all so we could have the peace found in his presence.

And peace within this change—and every change.

Dear Father in heaven, I thank you for your enduring presence that doesn't ebb and flow like waves in an ocean. Lord, I ask that you provide a clear sign of that presence with my child or loved one facing a mountain of change right now. It's hard enough for me to face my own change. It's excruciating to watch them have to do the same. Help me not swoop into savior mode but point them to you—the one true Savior. Any path this change makes them travel, may it bring them to a destination closer to you. You are worth it all. In the mighty name of Jesus, amen.

"Is prayer your steering wheel or your spare tire?" ~Corrie ten Boom

When I feel anxious and sorrowful over a loved one's change, I won't swoop in to save but sit with and support. I will accept that their change, like my own, brings some kind of good work and good lesson with it.

DAY 12

Divert Your Attention from Distractions

"Do not be worried and upset," Jesus told them.
"Believe in God and believe also in me."
John 14:1 GNT

I thought the gal next to me was a little overly invested in which bacon to buy.

But then again, I said to myself, *who am I to judge, really?* At that time, we sat smack-dab in the middle of a pandemic, and those were the days of being mindful and thankful for the small things. The last time I'd been at the store, right before the words *pandemic* and *coronavirus* became a part of our regular vernacular, there was no bacon at all. Today, the meat section was fully stocked. Whether to choose plain or black pepper or smoked applewood bacon? *Well,* I reasoned, *I could waffle over that choice too.*

When the bacon lady finally moved out of the way, I grabbed my own bacon (thick cut black pepper, thank you very much) and headed to the produce section. After picking up celery, carrots, two onions, and a lone leftover leek, I found a few needed nonperishables and made my way to the checkout lane. The young cashier and I engaged in a little small talk while I placed my items on the conveyor belt. When I'd finished, I scooted the cart toward the end of the aisle and opened my purse.

And that's when I noticed my wallet wasn't inside.

My heart dropped to my ankles as I repeatedly opened and closed and opened my purse again, thinking each time my wallet would surely reappear.

Not surprisingly, I thought the problem was with me. I asked the girl to set my groceries aside while I checked the car to see if I'd dropped it there. I speed-walked to the parking lot and scoured my car over and over, looking like a crazy person as I crawled all over my car, checking under seats and through the trunk to no avail.

I panic-called my husband to tell him what was going on, ending with a bemoaned, "I'm so stupid! How could I let this happen?"

After assuring me that I wasn't stupid and that these things just happen, my INTJ, levelheaded good man pointed out a possibility I never thought of: "Maybe someone took it when you weren't looking. Ask a manager to watch the security footage and see if they notice anything suspicious."

I couldn't have been more shocked if my husband had told me that coronavirus had suddenly vanished from the face of the earth. The idea that someone might've taken my wallet had never occurred to me.

After going back into the store and explaining the situation to the manager, I paid for my groceries (thank you, Apple Pay!) and waited on a metal folding chair while the manager viewed the security footage. Thirty minutes later, she confirmed that, indeed, my wallet had been stolen. While that gal took her sweet time choosing bacon in the meat department, a man reached into my purse, grabbed my wallet, and tucked it in his jacket. He, the bacon woman, and another man likely worked together.

The whole time, I'd only been a couple feet away from my purse—but was paying attention to the bacon lady.

Isn't it always the distractions that get us into trouble?

Later that night, after filing a police report online, I couldn't fall asleep for thinking about how I should've been watching my purse more carefully. At the same time, I knew I was dealing with two or three cohorts who played the game to take advantage of me, a game I didn't even know I was participating in. This was their doing—they set me up to fail. Still, I couldn't help feeling like I'd failed just the same.

While difficult change can come as a result of our own poor choices, it can also enter our lives as a result of other people's poor choices. Another's intentional plans can push us into a bad spot that sets us up to fail—that tells us we're failures. Whatever the case, the change is significant, leaving much loss in its wake—and anxiety that keeps us awake.

If that's you today, may I kindly turn you toward the warm light of hope and away from the distractions and anxiety change brings?

My friend Alli recently reminded me that we all fight a real enemy who daily strives to distract us from the Main Thing. On a phone call several weeks ago, she prayed this prayer with me:

We're at war with a real enemy right now. But you, God, are bigger than this enemy, and your presence is hope—the Way we fight for hope. Jesus says in the book of John, "Let not your heart be troubled." It's written in the imperative. It's a command. So, we confess and lay down our struggles and fears. We take up our marching orders to pray and hold fast to Jesus. Help us fight for hope by keeping our eyes fixed on you. Amen.

Friend, this is my prayer for you and me. As I tell my daughter, who's a new driver, "Keep your eyes on the road, because you steer where you see." Keep your eyes on hope, not the what-ifs of distractions that steal your peace.

Keep your eyes on Christ—and accept he is working through this change.

Keep your eyes on Christ—and accept he is working through this change.

We may not know when the struggles brought on by our change will end, but we know they *will* end. It may feel like this thing has set you up to fail, but you aren't a failure. And as you and I sit in the center of this change today, may we center ourselves in Jesus.

> You keep him in perfect peace whose mind is stayed on you, because he trusts in you. (Isa. 26:3)

I marched myself into the grocery store again last week, and as you can imagine, I was a heck of a lot more alert. I kept my purse on my arm instead of putting it in my cart. In the store, I'm not so distracted.

May the same be said outside the grocery store too.

Dear God of heaven, you know that difficult change handed to me by another person is particularly hard to accept. Thank you that while I didn't see it coming, you did. When our circumstances change, our story will not end there. Please show me how this change is your next best step for me. Remove any shame that tries to tell me I'm a failure, Lord, because I have victory in you. Help me fix my eyes on your Son, Jesus, in whose name I pray, amen.

"If you're lifting something heavy in your life, the Lord has allowed weight to be added to your life because by the power of God's Holy Spirit—not by your own strength—you'll keep faithfully lifting that weight. You have no idea how all the power that is in you is going to start taking shape outside of you. If there's resistance in your life right now, don't throw in the towel. Keep on lifting that weight because there is muscle coming to you that you would otherwise not have." ~Priscilla Shirer

Don't look at this change as a sign that you're a failure, and don't look at the distractions at all. Keep your eyes fixed on Jesus—and accept that he will carry you through this change.

DAY 13

Stay on the Track

Let perseverance finish its work so that you may be mature and complete, not lacking anything.

James 1:4 NIV

Born in Maryland as a slave in 1821, Harriet Tubman witnessed the cruel realities of slavery from a young age. In one such episode of inhumanity, at age fifteen, Harriet stood between an overseer and a fellow slave trying to escape, and as a result, the overseer struck her in the head with a two-pound counterweight.[1] For months following the attack, Harriet's life hung in the balance. She never completely recovered—the incident left a dent as well as a piece of metal in her skull.[2] For the rest of her life, she suffered from headaches as well as seizures that made her fall asleep at erratic times.

By 1849, Harriet could endure slavery no longer. With two of her brothers, she left their plantation at night to head for the Delaware border.[3] While her brothers eventually doubled back to the plantation, Harriet made it to Delaware and then onward to Pennsylvania.

Harriet could've rested content with her own freedom in the North, but she risked dangerous change to help others find freedom too. From Philadelphia, Harriet became one of the most active guides—or "conductors"—of the Underground Railroad. This distinction earned Harriet posted rewards for her capture of upwards of $40,000—equating to several million dollars today.[4]

After nineteen trips to the South and back, Harriet proudly claimed, "I was the conductor of the Underground Railroad for eight years, and I can say what most conductors can't say; I never ran my train off the track and I never lost a passenger."[5] She'd helped over three hundred slaves escape to freedom.

During the Civil War, Harriet worked for the Union army as a cook, nurse, and spy. She also led an armed expedition, the Combahee River Raid, and liberated more than seven hundred South Carolina slaves in the process.[6] She was the first woman to lead a major military campaign in the United States. After the war, Harriet continued to help veterans and former slaves.

In the 1890s, she underwent surgery in Boston to have the piece of metal in her skull removed. According to one account,

> She was offered anesthesia, but chose to bite a bullet instead, like she had seen so many Union soldiers do when their limbs were being amputated. In her own words, she said the doctor, "sawed open my skull, and raised it up, and now it feels more comfortable."[7]

When I review all Harriet encountered—slavery, a catastrophic blow to the head, seizures, many dangerous treks from South to North to South again, military battles, and getting through brain surgery by BITING A BULLET—well, I feel I need to reevaluate what I've considered actual "difficulties" in my own life. It's sobering to consider all this woman persevered through to bring as many people as possible to freedom.

Still, whether we're called to be a part of major historical change like Harriet or the smaller, unseen-by-the-world change in our own hearts and families, our assignment in accepting the change is the same: to trust that God will lead us through it.

That's what Harriet did. Regarding her successes, Harriet said, "Twant me, 'twas the Lord. I always told him, 'I trust to you. I don't know where to go or what to do, but I expect you to lead me,' and he always did."[8]

Whatever the scope, the Lord leads us through any change he brings in our lives.

Before passing away from pneumonia in 1913, Harriet said to those family and friends surrounding her bed, "I go to prepare a place for you."[9]

Harriet, whom God used to prepare a place at freedom's table for so many, finally met her Father in heaven who'd prepared a place for her.

Whatever the scope, the Lord leads us through any change he brings in our lives.

I don't know exactly what change is staring at you right now, but I do know that an important step in accepting it is resolving to persevere through it. And in persevering through it, we accept that God is using it as our own place of preparation. Our presence in and with this change has weight. It means something. It becomes the field in which we grow and mature into a sturdier tree that others can look at as a source of hope during their own changing trials.

Ellie Claire writes, "Take a new look at this season. Fight your frustrations, and trust that this place of preparation is of great importance."[10]

God is using this change to build you up and prepare you, and he will make known your next steps when you next need to know.

He doesn't compare your struggle with mine but asks us to see them as ways to prepare for our own assignments here on earth. Let's not miss the rewards perseverance brings because we got off the track too soon.

When change rattles each of us, we are called to "not be afraid or discouraged, for the LORD will personally go ahead of you. He will be with you" (Deut. 31:8 NLT).

Look back at Harriet's life and see.

Look into your own and know: the Lord has prepared a place for you.

Stay on the track and trust your Conductor to lead the way.

Lord, I'm jittery and nervous as I sit and wait to see what comes next during this difficult time of change. Show me what small adjustments I need to make so I can persevere through it—and accept it in the process. Show me how to stay on track so I complete the assignment you've given me. Help me be a light to another maneuvering a similar change. Thank you for loving us by giving us your only Son, whose saving grace makes up every tie of the railroad track. In his faithful name we pray, amen.

"I don't have a five-year plan. God's word is a lamp unto my feet, not my football field." ~Jamie B. Golden

I can more readily accept and persevere through change when I understand that God is using it as a place of preparation for me, one that is important and matters.

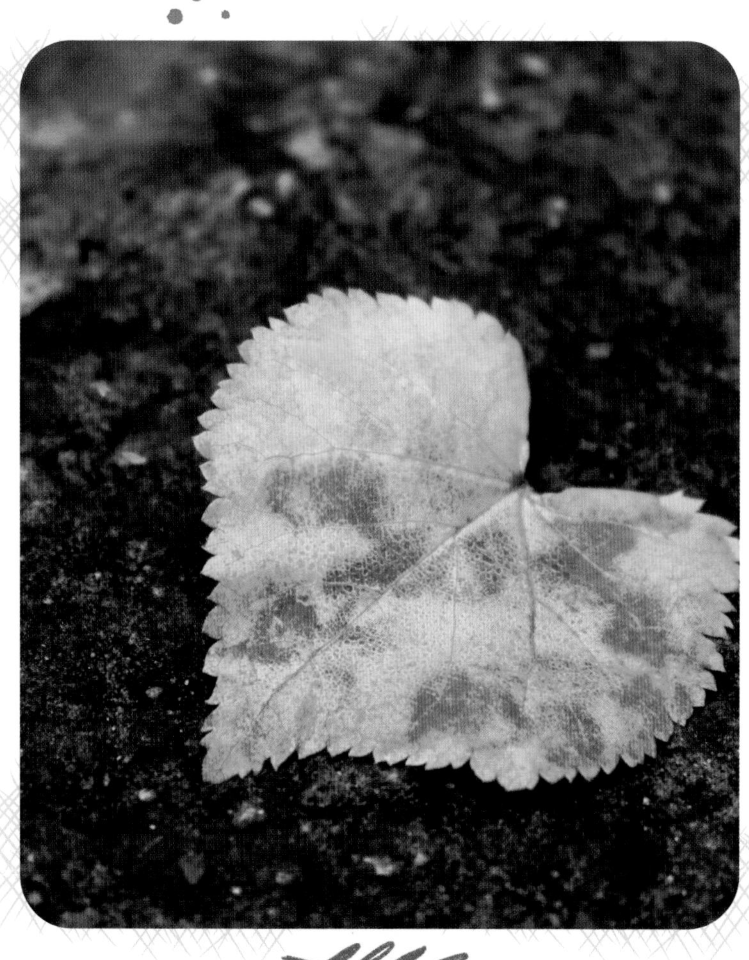

DAY 14

Love First, Know Second

So you see, our love for him comes as a result of his loving us first.

1 John 4:19 TLB

I met my husband, David, at Oklahoma State (Go Cowboys!), laying eyes on him for the first time when he joined the orchestra because we needed a few extra musicians for Beethoven's *5th Symphony*. He sat right behind me, and I'll just say it: I thought he was hot. I also thought he was way out of my league, so I settled on admiring him from afar. But because Jesus loves me this I know, David gave me a second and third look too. I found out later that he also liked to watch me walk across campus. My sister's then-boyfriend-now-husband told her the same thing.

What can I say? We O'Neill girls may have been born with crowded teeth and less than stellar vision, but we got that gait.

David and I began dating, and I fell fast and hard for this man who was a music lover, a hardworking student, and a man of strong convictions. However, I hesitated to tell my parents about this developing love story because of one main fact: I was eighteen, and David was twenty-six. As the oldest of three daughters, I knew that fact alone would be . . . how shall we say . . . not warmly received.

Eventually, I braved bringing up this new guy I was dating in a phone call with both my parents. When my mom asked me how old David was, I responded with the breeziness of someone on holiday in the Caribbean, "Ooohh, he's a junior." As a freshman myself, I thought that was honest without being *too* honest. And I got away with that answer for two, maybe three weeks. Eventually, though, my mom pressed me further about his age. "No, I don't want to know his grade level," she stated rather pointedly. "How old is he? As in, give me a *number*."

There was no hiding the whole truth anymore. I laid it all out on the table, and my poor daddy had a mini heart attack right then and there. Like most dads of daughters, he was automatically skeptical of any fellow we dated, and this twenty-six-year-old *man* was surely some kind of predator.

When I brought David home for the first time a month or two later, my dad was, conveniently, cleaning the shotgun at the kitchen table. Dad, who was known in our neck of the woods as a Will Rogers of sorts who never met a man he didn't like, spoke not one word to David for two solid hours. He simply stared at him as he slowly, methodically turned that shotgun into the cleanest weapon west of the Mississippi.

My dad was a straight shooter (pun intended) who didn't have a hypocritical bone in his long, lanky body. Unlike me, *he* probably would've told his mama his girlfriend's actual age right off the bat.

We all know people who aren't this way—people who say one thing and mean or do another. And during the long nights when change keeps us wide awake, it can be easy to wonder if this particular change exists as proof God is the same—a duplicitous imposter who says one thing and does another.

When it came to his daughters dating, my dad seemed to employ the mantra "Know first, love second." Once the man sitting on the other side of his stare proved to be trustworthy, *then* he would love him. Or at least, tolerate him. But not a moment before.

That policy may have been well and good when it came to daughters' boyfriends, and really, there are other examples when it's ideal to move first from knowledge and second from love. But when a change comes into our life that doesn't make a lick of sense and we struggle to see any kind of good within it, it's helpful to remember that because God loves us, everything he does for us comes as an expression from that love.

Because God *loves first*, we can *know second*.

When we struggle to accept change, it's often because we keep trying to turn that around. But God does not trick us or manipulate us. He isn't codependent either. Because of his extraordinary love for us, we trust that this change is for us too. Psalm 28:7 tells us, "The Lord is my strength and my shield; in him my heart trusts, and I am helped."

Move out of God's love for you first and trust his faithful follow-through.

We place our trust in him—and he helps us.

Trust first in him, then believe his help is here. Move out of God's love for you first and trust his faithful follow-through.

Sometimes this is hard to receive, because as Max Lucado teaches, human love depends on the receiver of the love, and we all know we humans have fluctuating feelings. It's the receiver of our love who regulates the love. But God's love isn't regulated. We have no thermostatic impact on the love of God for us—it's born from within him *first*. His love isn't dependent on us. He chose to love us, so we don't have to fear losing it.[1]

Eventually, my daddy came around to love David, but that's because David proved that he genuinely loved me and cared for me as much as—if not more than—my dad did. He won Dad over with his faithful care for and attention to me, so Dad trusted David.

Trust the Lord to move out of his faithful care for and attention to you too.

Because he loves you first, you can know you'll make it through this change second.

Heavenly Father, whether a change is brand-new or popping back into my life from long ago, all I know is I'm afraid because it's hard for me to fully trust you in this. Please help flip my mind, heart, and soul around so I first look to regular reminders of your love for me and immediately know you are faithful to follow through. Help me to trust you first when I can't know outcomes. When I do this, I can then be assured that no matter the trials this change brings, your love will carry me through. In the loving name of Jesus, amen.

"Your plans are still to prosper, you have not forgotten us . . . even what the enemy means for evil, you turn it for our good and for your glory." ~Pastor Scott Sauls

When change comes that is hard to accept, accept a "love first, know second" policy. First trust God's love for you and be okay with knowing second why the change is here.

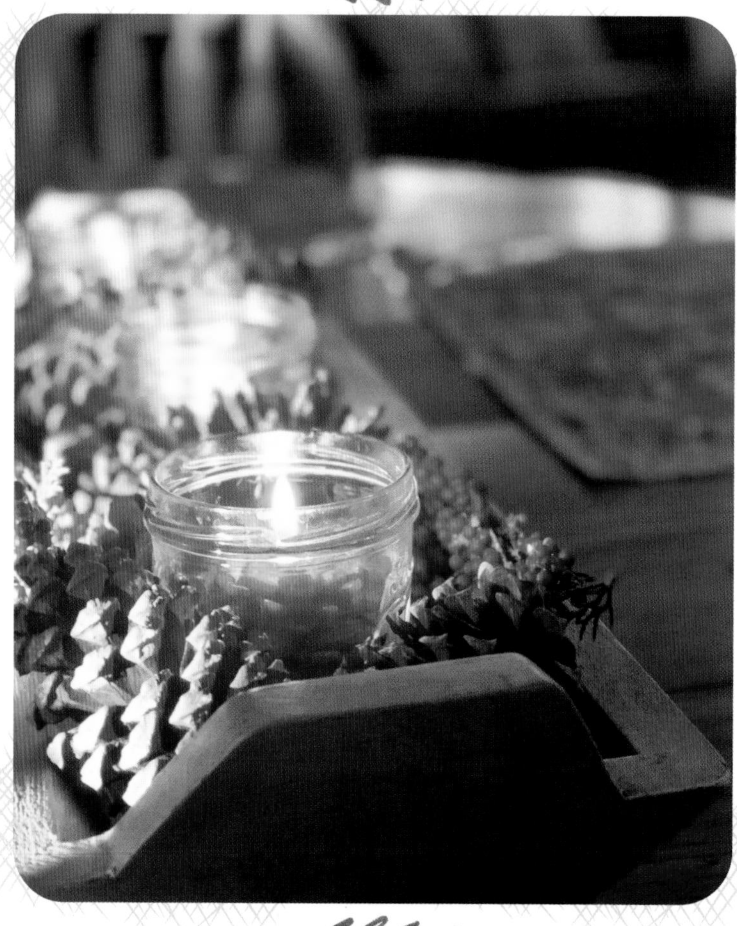

DAY 15

When Change Falls Darkest, Truth Blazes Brightest

We have this hope as an anchor for the soul, firm and secure.

Hebrews 6:19 NIV

When Kathy and Bill's daughter, Michelle, was a junior in high school, she began having severe swelling in her right calf. It wasn't constant, but when it was there it hurt to touch. While they inquired about it to their doctor several times, he never found anything wrong and only offered the same response: "She'll outgrow it."

But she didn't.

Michelle's calf started swelling more and more frequently, so on a Wednesday in November, Kathy and Bill once again took her to the doctor—a different doctor. After examining Michelle's leg, the doctor quickly left the room and returned with colleagues as well as a somber expression on his face. At that moment, he informed them that Michelle likely had a very serious tumor, and the treatment would probably be amputation.

The news knocked hard into Kathy, Bill, and Michelle, leaving them jarred and numb.

Change can do that to you—come right out of nowhere in the form of shattering news. It can make you feel so sick to your stomach you literally get sick. It can bring fear upon fear as every pained nerve jolts you wide awake to a new reality.

As they were a military family, the doctor planned to medically evacuate Michelle with her parents to the closest military hospital. But since this Wednesday was the day before Thanksgiving, that couldn't happen until the following Monday. So they left the doctor's office for home with that terrifying news sitting shotgun in the car.

That night, their church held a Thanksgiving Eve service, which the whole family attended. When they read the Scripture verse from their pew that evening, Hebrews 13:8, they felt the dark, heavy cloud surrounding them begin to ascend.

"Jesus Christ is the same yesterday and today and forever."

Immediately, Kathy and Bill were filled with God's peace as that Scripture blazed its way into their hearts and minds. Since Christ had been their foundation the day before the diagnosis, he was still their foundation on the day of the diagnosis. He would continue to be their sure footing for whatever happened in the future. When they comforted Michelle and talked to their sons about their sister's health crisis, this truth held them together as they prayed together and took care of one another.

Change can be a gift that brings hidden truth to light, truth that needs to be stared at and dealt with. That is, change can remove something unhealthy that you had no idea was unhealthy in the first place. At the

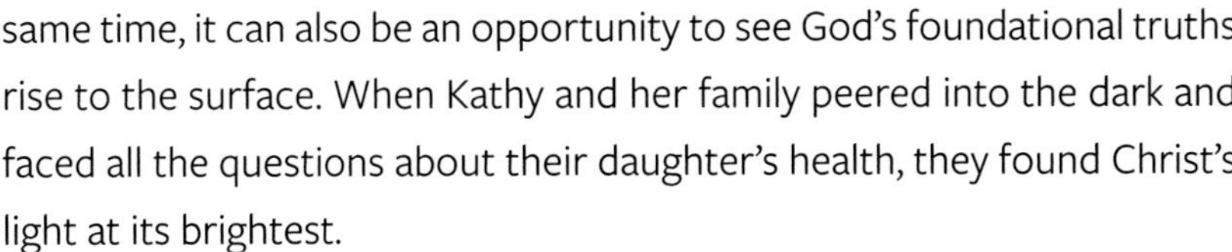

same time, it can also be an opportunity to see God's foundational truths rise to the surface. When Kathy and her family peered into the dark and faced all the questions about their daughter's health, they found Christ's light at its brightest.

In the first sentence of the second paragraph of Genesis, we read that God said, "Let there be light."[1]

> *Change can be a gift that brings hidden truth to light, truth that needs to be stared at and dealt with.*

God gave the world light, and then four thousand years later he moved as if to say once again, *Let there be light through the hope of the world.*

Epic change brought epic light—and epic hope.

As the light pierced the ebony night sky like a comet, Jesus came to have pierced hands so we could be saved from our helpless, dark condition. Jesus faced dark change head-on and stretched himself on the cross so we could be folded into his forever care. He came so we could see any unsettling change through the filter of his light and love.

God never lets death or destruction be the end of the story.

Within one of the darkest seasons for their family, Kathy and Bill clung to the light of that hope. Michelle's treatment, surgery, and recovery process were days filled with uncertainty and conflicting information. Their lives were upended and changed, but God remained consistent and unchanging—the same yesterday, today, and forever. Kathy and Bill felt Jesus's care as they folded themselves into Scripture and received reminders of God's sovereignty from family and friends. Their circumstances had dramatically changed, but their God had not. Even as Michelle was able, thankfully, to keep her leg, the lessons learned during that time about God's faithfulness served her and her family well through many future changes.

Dietrich Bonhoeffer said, "We must be ready to allow ourselves to be interrupted by God."[2] When God uses change to interrupt our lives, may we be like Kathy and Bill, who allowed the interruption by accepting the reality for what it was—and God's truth for what it is. May we too stand on God's faithful character and goodness. So, when change comes, we're settled in our souls that while change is ever present, so is God's unchanging presence.

Dear Father in heaven, I may not see what lies ahead within the darkness of this change, but I thank you that you do. And I thank you that you've given me Jesus, who went to the darkest places to bring the light of his saving presence. I thank you that because of this, any dark circumstances I face will not overcome me. I dread this change, but I know out of your great love for me it has exposed what needed the light. Help me stand firm on the foundational truth that Jesus has overcome the world and everything in it. Please fill me with the light of your peace and presence, Father God. I love you so. In the light-filled name of Jesus, amen.

"The Cross stands as the epitome of evil. And God takes the greatest evil ever known to humanity and turns it into the greatest Gift you have ever known. . . . If God can transfigure the greatest evil into the greatest Gift, then He intends to turn whatever you're experiencing now into a gift." ~Ann Voskamp, The Greatest Gift

Change can be the gift that brings hidden truth to light as well as what brings foundational truth to the surface, such as Jesus is the same today, tomorrow, and forever. While life is always changing, God's presence is not.

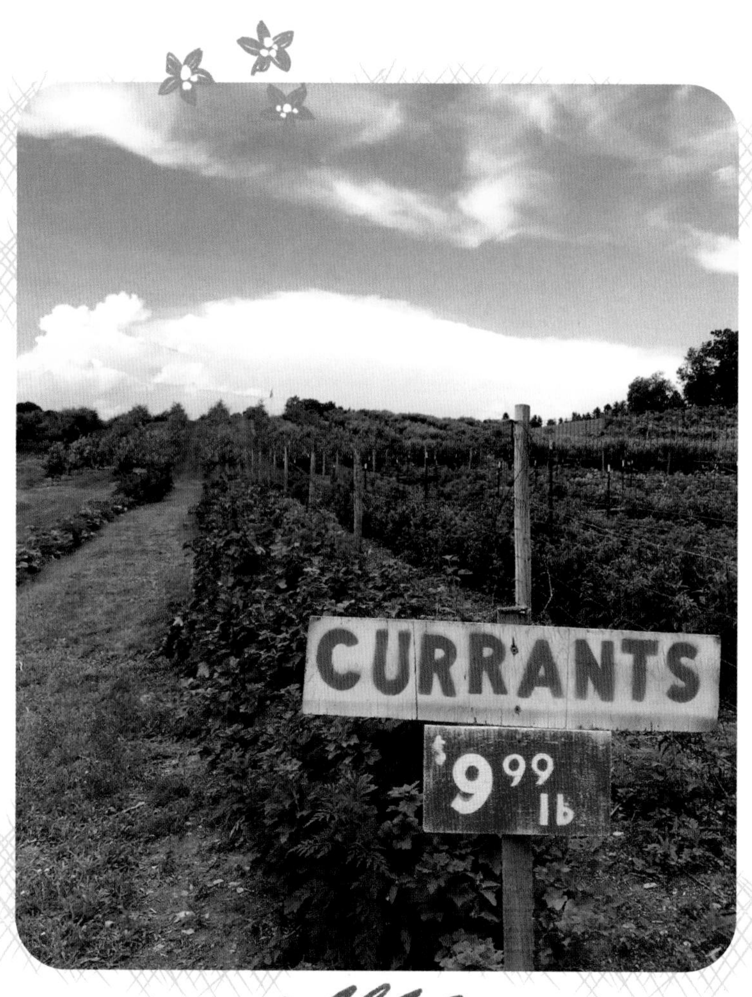
CURRANTS
$9.99
lb

DAY 16

Reach Further

And he is before all things, and in him all things hold together.

Colossians 1:17

Each month, I send out a monthly newsletter to a group of dear ones I affectionately refer to as "my porch people." Within the newsletter, I write a hodgepodge of "important nothings," to use an expression written by Jane Austen to her sister, Cassandra. I share more personal happenings from my neck of the woods that are important but not necessarily keeping the world spinning on its axis. Those important nothings could be what I share on coffee dates with Aimée or Maria or in Voxer conversations with Sara. It may be something painful like my sadness over the second anniversary of my dad's passing. Or it may be something lighthearted and inconsequential, like my love for the latest *Little Women* movie or Louise Penny novels.

Within my newsletters I include more private details about myself because my words are going to someone's inbox rather than out on the internet. And in return, I'm often blessed with readers who connect by sharing more personal details about their own lives with me.

In one of these recent newsletters, I told my porch people that I'd been working on a new book centered on my old friend change, and that if there was an aspect about change they would like to read about or learn from, I'd love it if they'd email me about it. I received responses of varying shades and tints, but one in particular stunned me still as a statue. A reader told me about losing her thirty-four-year-old daughter to leukemia, and the pain of no longer hearing her voice and her laughter. Struggling to get through the loss, she wrote, "Please include something in your book for mothers and fathers like me."

I immediately felt a burden to do just that. But at the same time, I felt ill-equipped to do so. What do you say to mamas and daddies who've been privileged to witness their child's story unfold for any duration of time, only to know it was cut short much too soon? What do you say to parents who've known the pain of burying their own heart with their child, yet still have to walk this planet in the slowest passing of time, feeling like a hollowed out human?

Because whether a child is lost at six seconds or sixty years, he or she is still a mama's baby, and any child lost before a parent is lost much too early.

Lately, I've thought so much about the beginning of Ecclesiastes 3, the passage where the expanse of time is shrunk down to several words:

> For everything there is a season, and a time for every matter under heaven:
>
> > a time to be born, and a time to die;
> > a time to plant, and a time to pluck up what is planted;

a time to kill, and a time to heal;
a time to break down, and a time to build up;
a time to weep, and a time to laugh;
a time to mourn, and a time to dance. (Eccles. 3:1–4)

The passage goes on to mention other life events and responses to them, and it strikes me that through much of life, we're in the middle of those events. But like a counterweight swinging out of control, a big change—like losing a child—can knock us into those bookend places of Ecclesiastes: weeping, mourning, dying. How . . . *when* will we ever feel centered again, know healing, laughing, and dancing again?

When we stand on the heart-wrenching side of those far-reaching pendulum moments, we remember we have the Father who carries us, Jesus who comes with us, and the Holy Spirit who comforts us. Sit with the Father who understands what it's like to lose a child. Depend on Jesus to see you through each day, and count on the Holy Spirit to tenderly lift you from the depths of your despair.

Writer Erin Moon says,

> In Christ, God is uniting all things. . . . Birth and death and everything in between. Planting and harvesting and everything in between. What's comforting here is that in the war, in the hate, in the losing, in the throwing away, in the weeping, in the breaking down, in the mourning; we are still being united in Him. Those pendulum swings do not knock us out of contention; they don't push us past a limit of His purpose. We can hold the tension because Christ is holding us.[1]

In the worst of trials brought on by change, Jesus still holds us and our loss—and helps us be able to accept it.

Dear one who's encountered unfathomable change such as the loss of what was most precious to you, I want you to know God sees you. I want you to know Jesus will sustain you. And I want you to know the Holy Spirit comforts you.

In the worst of trials brought on by change, Jesus still holds us and our loss—and helps us be able to accept it.

I want you to know your loss matters because your child's life matters.

Like a conductor in front of a full symphony orchestra, the Lord will one day unite all of our life experiences into one final, tonic note. All those important nothings, the devastating somethings, and the expansive space between will go from dissonance to resolution in one satisfying note. Let that knowledge do its slow work to turn hope-gone into hope-dawn.

Until that time comes, know your timeline for mourning this loss is just that: yours. Don't let others rush you through it because they're uncomfortable with your grief. Don't let others shame you because they think you're not handling it as well as you should be. Yes, there comes a time when we need to accept our loss. As you work on reaching that place, remember time on its own won't be what gets it done—but time spent with the Father, Son, and Holy Spirit will get you there.

Almighty God, you know as a parent what it's like to experience the devastating loss of a child. You know how our hearts split in two over such gargantuan losses in our life. Thank you for carrying us through the loss. Thank you that Christ cares for us along the way, and thank you for the comforting presence of the Holy Spirit. May I feel their presence in especially powerful ways as I move through this week, this month, and this year. Turn whatever hope-gone I have into hope-dawn—help me see what you see as you unite everything together for a hopeful purpose. In the everlasting name of Jesus, amen.

"Sorrow is one of the things that are lent, not given. A thing that is lent may be taken away; a thing that is given is not taken away. Joy is given; sorrow is lent. We are not our own, we are bought with a price, and 'our sorrow is not our own.' It is lent to us for just a little while that we may use it for eternal purposes. Then it will be taken away and everlasting joy will be our Father's gift to us, and the Lord God will wipe away all tears from off all faces. So let us use this 'lent' thing to draw us nearer to the heart of Him who was once a Man of Sorrows." ~Amy Carmichael, Edges of His Ways

In those moments when change is hardest to accept—when it has flung you into the far-reaching edge of the pendulum swing—you have the Father who carries you, Jesus who comes with you, and the Holy Spirit who comforts you.

ADAPT YOUR HEART TO BE FLEXIBLE,
BECAUSE GOD'S PLANS ARE PURPOSEFUL.

DAY 17

Put On the High-Waisted Pants

Oh, continue your steadfast love to those who know you, and your righteousness to the upright of heart!

Psalm 36:10

As I readied myself for church one Sunday, I pulled a new pair of jeans from the closet—wide-legged jeans with a super high waist. They're on trend, people, and I'm here for them in every way. As I zipped up this blessed piece of clothing all the way north of my belly button, I thought, *Where have you been the last twenty years?* They buttoned up my tummy and covered a multitude of stretch marks in the process.

I paired those jeans with a turtleneck, and I asked my husband what he thought of my ensemble. He said I looked good—like a Charlie's Angel. My son walked into the room, looked me up and down, then asked if we were taking the VW bug to church. (Note: we do not own a VW bug.)

I laughed to high heaven. What's a mama gotta do to get a little respect around here?

My family's insistence that I looked like I fell out of the seventies couldn't deter my delightful mood. I wore those pants like a Jaclyn Smith wannabe and enjoyed every minute of it. Goodbye, dissected muffin top! No spare tire overhang in these here parts. Glory be! I could wear those pants every day of the week.

Alas, what works in pants won't always work in principle.

The next day, I wore my regular ol' jeans and my regular ol' habit of running behind in my effort to get out the door on time to meet a new friend, Maria. Arriving at the coffee shop, I found her sitting at a central table. I couldn't help but also notice this military wife's kind blue eyes and strong frame acquainted with maneuvering a thousand responsibilities while her husband worked halfway around the globe. As we sat and sipped a chai latte and apple cider, respectively, I leaned into her tender demeanor and attentive way. Talking with her came easily.

At one point in our conversation, I told her of my struggle involving a new situation going on in my life. She listened thoughtfully. Then Maria proceeded to home in on the crux of my issue, to name it with such accuracy that I was a little stunned. She followed that up with her holy perspective on the whole thing, and I felt a wash of relief that made me tear up right then and there.

While I can be an open book of sorts and share easily, I don't usually do so until I've processed things on my own a good while. I almost never share really vulnerable stuff with someone I just met. I stay buttoned up and definitely don't get emotional. But this new friend's words just hit me square on the heart, and all my usual first-coffee-date protocol flew out the door into the chilly Colorado air.

Sometime later, a different matter altogether weighed me down, and I started to feel like I had an emotional muffin top of sorts. The matter squeezed me tighter and tighter, and finally, a little too suffocated from the whole thing, I said to my longtime friend Aimée, "Can I just ask you a really insecure question?" She answered, "Of course!" I did, and she immediately reassured me that the situation wasn't as bad as I thought it to be. Furthermore, after talking down my fears, she asked if she could ask *me* a really insecure question. I happily obliged.

While this close friend had been in my life for years, I'd never asked her a vulnerable question in such a direct way. But I was so glad I ignored my typical longtime-friend-coffee-date protocol and asked it anyway. By the end of that conversation, we both felt a little more like our usual selves, exhaling in our roomier pants.

After mulling over both these encounters, a few things occurred to me.

First, sometimes my ability to accept and adapt through the change in my life is directly proportional to the state of my near and dear relationships. Yes, there's a time and a place to keep our emotions buttoned up and on the inside. But we need friends who aren't turned off by or afraid to see those emotional muffin tops hanging over. We need a gal pal or two who willingly answers our insecure, dumb questions. We need dearies whose words and demeanor hold up a mirror to show us a more accurate reflection of ourselves. We need folks who'll redirect us to truth, the compass that keeps us from veering too far inside our own thoughts and fears.

Second, while we all have limited time and resources, I hope we remain open to meeting new people, because you and I never know where a simple coffee date might lead. Furthermore, we don't know how one insecure question could ease our burdens. It's a little scary to travel toward unfamiliar places, I know. But sometimes change asks us to wade through the uncomfortable waters of unfamiliarity to dive deep into God's rest and healing. First Samuel 2 says this in the Message translation: "He protectively cares for his faithful friends, step by step, but leaves the wicked to stumble in the dark. No one makes it in this life by sheer muscle!" (v. 9).

God may confirm his will for you and affirm his love for you through someone you know well or less than well, but he will speak to you through another. So, when you're looking to settle into and adapt to your change, you want to be in the position to have a wise friend or loved one in the vicinity from whom you can catch a clearer vision of what the Lord has in mind for you next.

Persist in proximity to others and perceive the promises of God.

Persist in proximity to others and perceive the promises of God.

Dear one, wear those high-waisted pants as much as you please. But don't waste those emotional muffin top moments, especially those that come with change. Let them be arrows pointing you toward a little vulnerability with a safe person who lets you exhale. They see you in the same light as Jesus sees you. They don't dissect every little unattractive problem you have.

They let you wear those high-waisted pants . . . and tell you how good you look in them too.

Dear Father God, thank you that you are our safest place to be vulnerable. Thank you for your Son, who selflessly followed your will so we could be saved and sanctified. Lord, you know the reason I may struggle with vulnerability during this season of change. Will you bring to my attention just one person I could share a struggle with—someone who could show me a glimpse of how you see me? Thank you for welcoming all of me into your presence: fears, flaws, failures, and all. In the mighty name of Jesus, who loved me while I was still a sinner, amen.

"The Holy Spirit is here to guide us. The two tools of the Spirit are the verse and the voice. The first place to go to is the verse—the Scripture. Then, oftentimes, God will affirm what you find in the verse with a voice, a word of wisdom from a seasoned friend or saint."
~Max Lucado

Sometimes, our ability to accept and adapt through the change in our life is directly proportional to the state of our near and dear relationships. Use your emotional muffin top moments as arrows pointing to the need to be vulnerable with someone safe in your life.

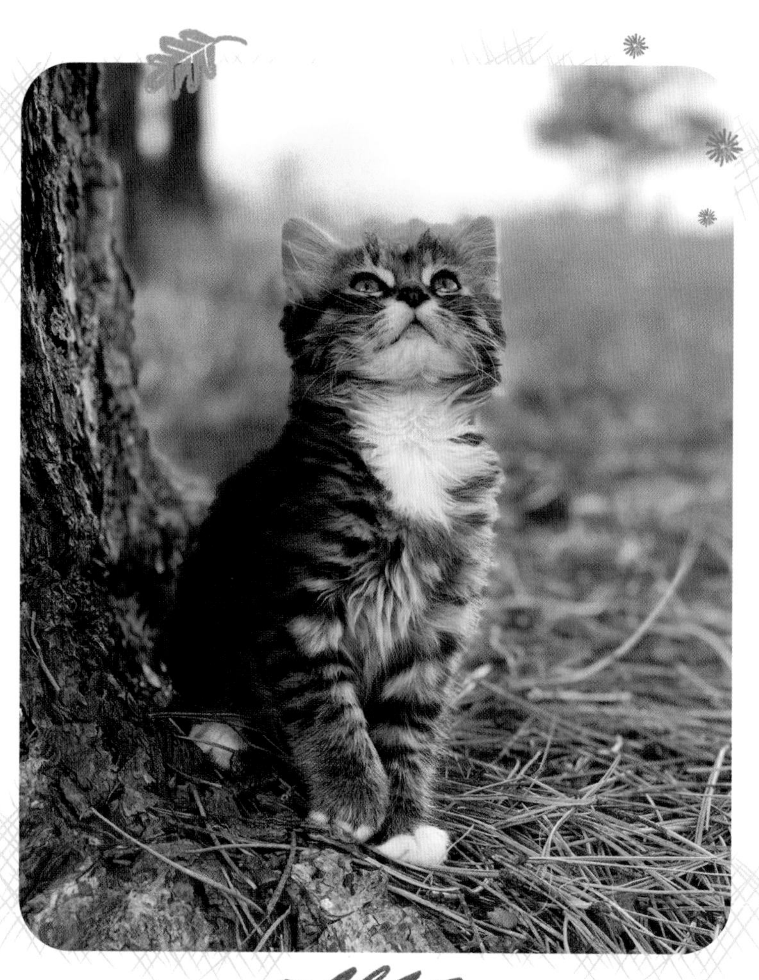

DAY 18

Get Uncomfortably Comfortable in Your Circle

Love one another with brotherly affection.
Outdo one another in showing honor.
Romans 12:10

Show hospitality to one another without grumbling.
1 Peter 4:9

I still remember landing at the small island airport in Hawaii for the first time, walking hand-in-hand with our four-year-old daughter toward the baggage claim. I was exhausted after the long flight and terribly nervous about this big life change, about finding my place and people there. Sure, we were stationed in paradise, but would my friendship landscape look more like a desert? At our previous assignment, it took me well over a year to make one local friend. And by the time I made a few, it was time to move again.

At that airport, our eight-year-old sons searched for a luggage cart while my husband and I guessed whether or not it would hold all ten bags. And that's when I looked up and saw over a dozen men and women walking toward us with smiles as warm as the trade winds. Members of David's new detachment, along with several family members, had come to welcome us to the island.

A married couple, Mark and Kim, introduced themselves and placed candy leis around the kids' necks. Kim placed a lei of kukui nuts around David's neck and a lei of orchid flowers around my own.

I smelled the fragrant purple flowers and felt their tender blooms, enlivened and encircled by these folks' kind gesture.

We moved into our home two days before Thanksgiving, so our holiday season that year held more garlands of packing tape than greenery. Still, Mark and Kim made a space for us in their own festive home, inviting us over for Thanksgiving dinner as well as for dessert Christmas night. I remember that warm Christmas evening, licking orange Bundt cake frosting off my fingers. In more ways than one, it was a sweet punctuation mark at the end of a hectic, demanding holiday season.

A decade later, I also see it as the beginnings of a dear friendship, one that remains a safe place for me to share the good, bad, and ugly going on in my life.

In those days of moving every few years, anxiety over finding community for my family and me rode shotgun with every transition. Sometimes I found it easily, as with Kim. Many times, I did not. That anxiety can still show up, albeit for different reasons. And quite frankly, it frustrates the living daylights out of me.

When it comes to this discussion of belonging and community, *vulnerability* is a sparkly, catchy word. I've heard so many say something along the lines of "We must refuse the tendency to isolate ourselves and share the real stuff." Well, yes. I get it—that's true. However, the desire to share vulnerably is only half of the picture.

For me to share vulnerably, I need someone to offer me a safe place to be vulnerable.

Now, some will automatically point out that it's my responsibility to put myself out there and introduce myself to others so I'm in the best position to meet new folks. And they would be right. But the fact is, it's not all up to me. Whether you're moving to a new place or through a new life stage or anywhere in between, you may see hard proof that all the people around you have their people. If I have a heart willing to share, how do I break in to share my struggles when I can't find a space to do so?

For me to share vulnerably, I need someone to offer me a safe place to be vulnerable.

I've had people write me off before, and I know I've done the same to others. Sometimes that's because of a good reason, like we just didn't click. Plus, we all have limited bandwidth in our day and must give our time and attention to whom God asks.

But sometimes—and I think this occurs more frequently than we'd like to admit—we get comfortable with our people, and we don't want to take the time and energy to widen our own circles.

As someone who's lived in Colorado Springs for ten years now, I certainly can't claim to be the new person. As much as anyone, I fight this tendency to travel the well-worn roads of familiar relationships rather than brave the potentially bumpy, uncomfortable road to a new one. I fight the urge to tap the "cruise control" button and coast along near those friends with whom I comfortably sit today.

If, like me, you find yourself in a blessed life stage with a treasured posse of people around you, I encourage you to keep your eyes and heart open to widening your circle just the same. We'll never "arrive" at finding our place and people. It's more an ever-winding road than a destination.

And if you're where I've been, still trying to find your people in your place, I encourage you to not give up. The Lord absolutely wants you to have those with whom you can vulnerably share. But like the farmer who must work long and hard before the harvest, it may take a frustrating amount of time.

In times chock-full of calm *or* change, we can adapt to the idea that God is always doing a new thing for each of us. Isaiah 43:19 says,

> Behold, I am doing a new thing;
>   now it springs forth, do you not perceive it?
> I will make a way in the wilderness
>   and rivers in the desert.

May we all get a little uncomfortably comfortable in reaching out to someone else—even in the smallest of ways. Because it's in the reaching out that God may show us the new good thing he wants to give us.

May we be in some small way ever ready to widen our circles, welcome another in, and help kick anxiety from change out of the shotgun seat for someone else.

Dear Lord, thank you for placing me where I am. Even if my friendship landscape currently looks more desert than tropical island, I know that I'm not here accidentally. And since you specialize in turning dry deserts into lush gardens, I believe you will show up for me as your grace and good will determine. Lord, show me my place and people who will help me through this change. And if I'm a little too comfortably settled in, help me see someone for whom I can create a safe place to be vulnerable too. In Jesus's name, who's a Friend to all, amen.

"We have been invited into their lives, from which we will never be evicted, or evict ourselves." ~Wallace Stegner, Crossing to Safety

If I'm mindful in keeping my heart flexible, I can be more attentive to welcoming a new friend into my circle rather than strictly (and comfortably) engaging with the people who are already there. After all, the Lord is always doing a new thing, and that new person may in turn help me adapt through my own change.

DAY 19

Look for Jesus in Your Neighborhood

And God is able to make all grace abound to you, so that having all sufficiency in all things at all times, you may abound in every good work.

2 Corinthians 9:8

After cleaning the dishes and wrestling twin sons to bed, I flipped off their light and moved through the hallway toward the rocking chair in the living room. I grabbed one arm with one hand, slowly lowering myself into the chair from the side like pregnant women do. I was plumb exhausted. David was out of town, and the boys' never-ending energy was a lot to wrestle on my own. I was also wrestling with the news my OB told me, news that brought a whole new kind of change to my life.

While I carried twins with nary a problem, this second pregnancy with my daughter had been problematic from the get-go. Since she wasn't growing as she should, and I had extra physical problems to boot, I'd been placed on partial bedrest. Unlike full bedrest, I had permission to sit, stand,

and walk around for short periods of time. Modified though that may be, I was still trying to figure out how that was going to work with two always-on-the-move three-year-old sons and a husband who was gone as much as he was home. Since the doctor didn't put me on full-blown bedrest, I couldn't justify asking family to come in from out of town to stay with me. Still, according to the doctor, I must limit all unnecessary activity and not pick up or hold the boys.

I laughed in my chair till I started crying. I mean, how does one mind doctor's orders when you're largely the only adult in the house and your twin sons relish making a sport of regularly sprinting in opposite directions?

I prayed for the Lord to show me a way through what seemed an impossible situation. I soon discovered his answers came not through a plan or a procedure but through the beloved people who lived in my neighborhood.

Mary asked what groceries I needed, and she brought them all, including fun treats not on my list like ice cream and dark chocolate. Elisabeth brought me weekly meals, no small chore with a busy husband and five young children of her own to cook for. Rebecca regularly had my boys over to play with her son. Jen kept me company after she got off work, and Cheryl brought me caffeine-free sweet tea with lemon, the treat of all treats. I downed it with joy while entertained by her humor and wit as my kids were entertained by hers.

My people came hour by hour, day by day, and helped me through.

Those dear neighbors and friends carried me in a thousand ordinary ways, and in doing so God carried me to the thirty-eighth week of my pregnancy, when I delivered a tiny but healthy 5 lb. 4 oz. baby girl.

I had expected help to arrive through my husband's schedule suddenly relaxing or Grandma and Grandpa swooping through the front door, or maybe even through resources provided by my church. I thought help would be some kind of packaged deal that would look the same day in, day out. When he was home, my husband certainly did his part as co-parent. But David had an important job to do that paid the bills, so he couldn't be home all the time. Sometimes I asked for the help I needed, but more often than not, what I remember is my neighborhood posse gathering what I needed and doing a hundred small-but-big things to fill the gaps.

They became what I needed when I needed it, not unlike the friends of the paralyzed man who parted the crowd in front of Jesus when they lowered him from the roof. They had tried the more conventional, logical route—through the front door—the first time. But eventually they settled on plan B, and Jesus healed the man in front of everyone (Luke 5:17–20).

When we're going through a major change, we can't always count on what might be the most "logical" plan or procedure to be how help arrives. More often than not, we won't see the long-term view of a solution, nice as that would be. But God often shows up for us through people, people who provide hour by hour, day by day help when we need it. People who provide hopeful words as well as practical action.

God is able to make all grace abound to us, yes, but we often want it to apply to all the rest of our days. Instead, God gives us enough grace for this hour. Today. He'll give us enough for tomorrow too. But we can't borrow tomorrow's against today just so we feel better or more in control. Change reminds us we have no assurances in what we will find in the future, but it can't change the fact that God's grace is assured to us each day.

If your circumstances are such that you're sitting at a dry well on the people front, this I know: God will not leave you there. He will bring you what you need when you need it. It may be a steady reveal, where your needs are fulfilled slowly yet surely. But the Lord will make a way for you to get through this change. And you and I will adapt well through change when we stay open and flexible to help arriving when and where we don't necessarily expect it. Look in your neighborhood—literally and figuratively. God is working while you're waiting.

God is working while you're waiting.

He helped David adapt to change through Jonathan (1 Sam. 18:1–5).

He helped Ruth adapt to change through Naomi (the book of Ruth).

He helped Mary adapt to change through Elizabeth (Luke 1:39–45).

And he helped Kristen adapt through Cheryl, Elisabeth, Jen, Lisa, Mary, Rebecca, and others still.

He'll help you too.

Dear Father in heaven, I thank you, first and foremost, for giving me what I need when I need it. You see every detail of my situation, and you will provide for me in this circumstance. You see the exact kind of help I need. While it's right and good for me to look for help in expected places, give me the wisdom, direction, and creativity to look in unexpected places too. Remove any unbelief within me and help me to have faith fully in you. Your power will be made perfect in my weakness. In Jesus's name, amen.

"Be still my soul the Lord is on thy side
Bear patiently the cross of grief or pain
Leave to thy God to order and provide
In every change He faithful will remain
Be still my soul thy best, thy heavenly friend
Through thorny ways leads to a joyful end."
~Katharina von Schlegel, "Be Still My Soul"

During times of change, God will bring you the help you need day by day, from both expected and unexpected places. This support will help you adapt to change.

DAY 20

Consider God's Redirection

God knows what's going on.
He takes the measure of everything that happens.
1 Samuel 2:3 Message

One of my favorite childhood memories involves my family gathering around our RCA console once a year to watch *The Sound of Music* on network television. I still remember taking it in for the first time, lying on the dark carpet with my head propped up on green velvety pillows. By the end of the movie, I'd moved from the floor to my dad's lap, wondering if the von Trapp family would escape the Nazis or be discovered by them.

That initial viewing kicked off a love affair with that movie and its music. As a young kid, I was known to sweet-talk relatives into reenacting "So Long, Farewell" with me. I still sing "My Favorite Things" year-round, and if I ever met Julie Andrews I'd probably keel right over from sheer excitement.

Come to think of it, Captain von Trapp might've been the first fellow I thought looked good in a uniform.

Anyway.

Julie Andrews, who played the movie-musical's central character, Maria, has enjoyed a long career as a Broadway and screen actress. In the 1990s, Julie brought another movie role of hers, the lead in *Victor/Victoria*, to the Broadway stage. The success of that show meant Julie performed on Broadway many months longer than she had originally intended. As a result, Julie became quite vocally tired, and her vocal cords developed muscular striations, something that is rather common for Broadway singers. Julie underwent surgery to have tissue removed from her vocal cords, but sadly, it wasn't a successful operation. Julie faced one of the most difficult changes of her life: her four-octave vocal range was reduced to nearly nothing, and she lost the ability to sing as she had done all her life. A simple surgery to heal a voice strained from singing ended up becoming a life complication that stole that singing voice almost completely.

When asked if losing her voice was the greatest loss of her life, Julie answered that it was a huge one, and it took her quite some time to get through the loss. But today, Julie also says that closed door opened a different one she was able to walk through with her daughter Emma: writing books.

One day, as Julie lamented to Emma about how much she missed singing, her daughter turned to her and said, "Mum, you've just found a different way of using your voice."[1]

Together, Julie and Emma have published over thirty books, some of which are bestsellers. As Maria states in *The Sound of Music*, "When the Lord closes a door, somewhere he opens a window."[2]

This is not always fun or simple, but it's true: God might elect to do some reconstruction in your life—and in your heart. He may close off one door to make room for one in a better place, one that accounts for an extra window or two. But to adapt through it, you may need to reframe how you see the whole situation, reframe your view. And to reframe your view, you must remember that when the change in your life takes something away, God makes room for something better to take its place.

Where we get in trouble, I think, is believing a closed door is the end of things. It's final. Over. Done. And yes, I realize that in one way, that may be true. But what if the Lord allowed the change to be brought into our lives not as an end but as a redirection? When one door closes, can we look around us and see another one opening?

Paul of the New Testament knew the reality of this ending-turned-redirection very well. As he, Silas, and Timothy went out to preach God's Word throughout a particular region that God had directed them to enter, the Holy Spirit stopped them.

> They went to Phrygia, and then on through the region of Galatia. Their plan was to turn west into Asia province, but the Holy Spirit blocked that route. So they went to Mysia and tried to go north to Bithynia, but the Spirit of Jesus wouldn't let them go there either. (Acts 16:6–7 Message)

Even as God closed the door on Paul and his traveling companions' original destinations, he brought Paul a vision that clarified their journey:

> That night Paul had a dream: A Macedonian stood on the far shore and called across the sea, "Come over to Macedonia and help us!" The dream gave Paul his map. We went to work at once getting things ready to cross over to Macedonia. . . . We knew now for sure that

God had called us to preach the good news to the Europeans. (vv. 9–10 Message)

A big change can be a big redirection—not a termination. A big transition can lead to a refinement in how you'll use your voice, not the end of your voice altogether. It just requires you to reframe what you're looking at so you can see it in a new way.

Could the redirection bring a loss that needs mourning? Certainly. But when we reframe the loss in the light of God's purposeful plans for us, it can lead to new loves. We still might wish we'd never had to deal with the change at all. But when we keep our heart open and flexible enough to see it as an opportunity for something new, we deal with it and adapt through it. And with time, we may well learn that to be spared from the change may have brought short-term simplicity but long-term difficulty.

With time, we may well learn that to be spared from the change may have brought short-term simplicity but long-term difficulty.

In your own reframing moments of change, keep your eyes and heart open for a different door to walk through—or even crawl through if necessary. See the reframing in a way that takes the story God's working through you into account.

As you and I work to adapt through this change, may we be able to see our story within his-story. May we see it as a redirection that leads straight back to the heart of God, always beating *for* us.

Dear heavenly Father, if you close a door, it's only because you want to redirect my attention elsewhere—to a new door. You want to show me a different way through. Help me then, Lord, to adapt through this change by seeing the different possibilities you have in mind for me. Help me see the new direction you want me to travel. Help slow my anxious heart by staying my mind on this reframed picture. My own closed door may lead to a new destination or the same one as before. Either way, I trust you to lead me where I'm supposed to be. Thank you for your Son, Jesus, who goes with me along the way. In his name, amen.

"We didn't know that dreams coming true weren't always the best thing. That wasn't what the stories told."
~Patti Callahan, Becoming Mrs. Lewis

A big change isn't always the end of things but rather a direction refined. To adapt through it, reframe it.

DAY 21

What Change Can't Take Away

Steep your life in God-reality, God-initiative, God-provisions. Don't worry about missing out. You'll find all your everyday human concerns will be met.

Matthew 6:33 Message

Lately, I've been doing this tiny-yet-tremendous thing where I give up my beloved Instagram over the weekends. For years I've not had Facebook or Twitter on my phone, but that's really not a sacrifice because I could take or leave both of those. But Instagram? Well, your girl here loves her some Instagram. I never thought seriously about giving it up till I heard my friend Lisa-Jo mention that actress Tracee Ellis Ross gives it up—and her 7.5 million followers—on the weekends. While I've never entertained giving it up altogether, it never occurred to me that I could explore a "middle of the road" option and take a break from it for a small amount of time.

What also surprises me is the jolt of joy doing so provides. Yeah, sometimes I have to pop on for a work "to-do," but (so far) I'm able to do what needs doing without mindless scrolling. Giving up Instagram on the weekends helps me tip the scales from FOMO (Fear of Missing Out) to JOMO (Joy of Missing Out). Each Monday morning, I add it back and start the week from a tank full of all the best stuff: my real-life family and friends.

Generally, I don't miss whatever I've missed out on.

But on one particular Monday, I manage to see a smattering of posts about folks who are meeting without me, and daggum it, my good mood tanks right next to my perceived sliding social status. As I stare at the picture of happy faces, I understand that it's not really the fact that they got together that bothers me. I don't know if I would've even wanted to go—but let me tell you this for sure: I wanted to be asked. A couple of years ago, I *would've* been asked, but today that's clearly different. And that change hurts.

I surprised myself at how strongly this change made me feel—a bit like some kind of lesser-than disappointment whom others don't want to put up with.

This smacks me hard on a Monday, but come Tuesday, I've gained a little ground back the way many of us do: by taking care of what needs taking care of right in front of me. In doing this, I bring my world down to where I am today. So, I clean the kitchen counters. I bake chocolate chip cookies. I zigzag across town mailing packages and buying groceries. I write a few words for my blog and text my sons, who are at the college campus up north. Bit by bit, the more I settle into my current view, the more I expand my belonging—no matter the change.

But I'm not so above my struggles with sadness or my awareness of this change in belonging that I don't recognize another fact about change: it can be greedy. More accurately, the enemy can use change to manipulate us into thinking all it's here to do is take, take, take.

I've believed headstrong change wants to reach its hands beyond any kind of reasonable boundary and hungrily take more than its share. Again, this exposes my tight fists of control and expectations and reveals the real problem: my inability to trust and believe that God is not working around this change for me but is working smack-dab through the middle of it for me.

God is not working around this change for me but is working smack-dab through the middle of it for me.

In our work to adapt through the change in our lives, we can't make it harder than it already is by allowing the enemy to convince us it's only here for the taking. It seems a good place to start is to take our eyes off what we're missing and train them toward what we're getting. When I do this, I firmly tell change that it will not widen my view so far out that I see too many people and places God never intended for me to belong with in this season.

But this is still true for you and me, no matter the season: God intends for us to belong somewhere—he always wants us to belong where we are, no matter what change we're facing.

Hebrews 13:12 tells us, "So Jesus also suffered outside the gate in order to sanctify the people through his own blood."

Jesus knew what it was to be on the outside, but he wasn't on the outside looking in. He was on the outside looking up. He suffered so we could be sanctified.

We can also know that when we suffer because of change, we're being sanctified. It's not in our lives for nothing—it's here to teach us something. So, as we listen and learn, we can model Jesus, the founder and perfecter of our faith, who didn't let people's wishy-washy, fickle natures keep him from looking only to God with expectation.

I think about this the rest of that week, all the way to Friday, which is a long day with my daughter's evening activities. She and I arrive home late into the evening, tired and ready for stretchy pants and Netflix.

Just when we start to watch a show, the doorbell rings. I look to my husband, eyebrows coming together.

"Who in the world could that be?"

He gives me a sly smile. "I don't know, but why don't you open the door and find out?"

I peek into the peephole, turn around with silver-dollar eyes, and say, "No! Really?!?" Then I open the door and my mouth drops open as I take in the view of my two tall twin men-children, flooded in porchlight.

James says, with eyes lit up, "Hey, Mama! We're home for the weekend! Did we surprise you?" Ethan just smiles country mile–wide and wraps a long arm around my shoulders.

I'm breathless with joy—and the good kind of change. If I could, I'd order it up every weekend.

"YES!" I shout while hugging their necks clean off. "Yes! And it's the best kind of surprise I could ever receive!"

The Monday of that week is a distant memory. What I perceived to be missing is a distant memory too. I'm wide awake to what I'm receiving: an expansive place to belong in the middle of change.

Dear Father God, I know that since you care about the sparrows having what they need, you certainly care about me having what I need. Lord, when the enemy tries to tell me this difficult change will only take, take, take, be the loudest voice I hear calling it hogwash. Infuse me with a spirit of contentment and wide-awakeness to the good change gives. Show me all the ways I belong right here, right now. Help me adapt through this change by clinging to Jesus, your Son, who took his place on the outside so I could forever be on the inside. In his gracious good name, amen.

"God's will for our lives is less about where we go, and more about who we are." ~Dominic Done

Don't let the enemy convince you change only takes good from you. Change gives good too. Model Jesus, who wasn't on the outside looking in but on the outside looking up, and know that change cannot remove God's desire and plans for you to belong.

DAY 22

Failure Can't Knock You Off Course

At the right time, I, the LORD, will make it happen.

Isaiah 60:22 NLT

Lonnie Johnson grew up in Mobile, Alabama, tinkering with materials and building rockets as a young child. In 1968, he built a robot named Linex out of scrap metal, which he and his school's science team took with them to compete at the University of Alabama's science fair. Desegregation had occurred only five years prior. Lonnie and his classmates were the only Black students competing, so the campus's unwelcoming, hostile atmosphere was the *real* challenge of the science fair.[1]

Nevertheless, Lonnie and his team won first place at the fair—the first in a long line of scientific achievements for Lonnie. In spite of being told he could never advance beyond "technician" in the field of science, Lonnie attended the Tuskegee Institute and became an engineer. He went on to NASA, where he worked in their jet propulsion laboratory and as a systems engineer for the *Cassini* mission to Saturn and the *Galileo* mission to Jupiter.[2] Lonnie faced skepticism over finding a way to create a constant source of power supply for the *Galileo* orbiter and probe, but he didn't let that deter his efforts. As a result, Lonnie successfully developed a power package that allowed the *Galileo* to photograph Jupiter and its moons.[3]

Always tinkering, Lonnie invented a water-propelled toy airplane, two kinds of engines, and an environmentally friendly cooling system for refrigerators and air conditioners that used water instead of freon. While testing that cooling system, Lonnie aimed a nozzle at his bathtub and pulled the lever of his prototype. He was shocked to see a powerful water stream blast right into the bathtub.[4]

Eventually, Lonnie quit his day job as an engineer to become a full-time inventor and pitched his many product prototypes to toymakers and interested investors. While there was interest in his inventions, plans for expanding and selling each item fizzled out. Eventually, Lonnie had no job and no money, and he and his family had to move out of their home and into a small apartment.

It was hard to believe that the man who had worked as a rocket scientist for NASA struggled as he did.

Still, Lonnie kept after it. For seven long years, Lonnie refined his inventions and sought investors. Finally, the Larami Corporation bought his "Power Drencher" device. After some marketing improvements and a name change, the "Super Soaker" was born and went on to be one of the world's top twenty selling toys in 1991.[5]

Following his success with the Super Soaker, Lonnie founded the Johnson Research & Development Company. One of the functions of this R & D company is acquiring patents, including one for the Johnson

Thermoelectric Energy Converter (JTEC), a sophisticated heat engine that converts solar energy into electric energy.

Lonnie's story of hard work, determination, and strong belief in the talents God gave him shows us this: the failures of change will not deter God's plans for you and where you're supposed to be.

The failures of change will not deter God's plans for you and where you're supposed to be.

Sure, you can struggle because people tell you what you want to do isn't available for you. You can sweat and toil and fight incredible odds for years—to no avail. From the outside, your circumstances may have you thinking, *Let's just call it what it is: failure.* The dream is dashed. The idea is a wash. You used to have what it took to succeed, but not anymore. At some point, you face facts that hope is gone.

You face facts that the change in circumstances is here to stay.

And then, all of a sudden, the Lord makes a way through it you never could've anticipated, like he does in the book of John.

After a long day of watching Jesus heal people and perform miracles, including the feeding of the five thousand, his disciples went down to the Sea of Galilee and stepped into a boat to travel to Capernaum. Jesus was lollygagging behind, and a strong wind came up and the seas became rough. The disciples rowed three or four miles before seeing Jesus walking on the water toward them. They became frightened, to which Jesus replied, "It is I; do not be afraid" (John 6:20). Relieved, the disciples helped him into the boat. At that time, Scripture proceeds to tell us the most amazing thing: "Then they were glad to take him into the boat, and immediately the boat was at the land to which they were going" (v. 21).

Dear one, as you and I move along through life, we will meet changes in the form of storms. They will annoy us, terrify us, and do their level best to steer us off course. They will make us question what we're doing out in the boat in the first place. As you fight to stay true to God's path for you, remember this: the Lord will get you where you're supposed to be. He isn't aimless, directionless, or careless; he isn't merely along for the ride. He is purposeful, powerful, and faithful. You can persevere through this because God's presence persists in this. No EF5 tornado or category 5 hurricane will change his course of direction in your life.

Keep using the talents God's given you to move in the direction he guides you. Hold on to the realization that failure is not the end destination. When change knocks you off course, remember this: hope always gets the last word, and the Lord will get you where you're supposed to be.

Heavenly Father, thank you that no change can thwart your design and intention for my life. Thank you that you go with me and get me where I'm supposed to be. When it's hard to see beyond my failure, give me a hopeful vision of what the future may bring so I persevere and push through. Give me a peaceful heart that adapts to the future you have set out before me. In the redeeming name of Christ, amen.

"Courage is going from failure to failure without the loss of enthusiasm." ~Winston Churchill

Failures will come, yes. But no matter how the failures of change stir up your life or knock you off course, the Lord will get you where you're supposed to be.

Abide

ABIDE IN JESUS BY LEANING INTO THE CHANGE HE ALLOWS.

DAY 23

Lean into Breath Prayers

My people will abide in a peaceful habitation,
in secure dwellings, and in quiet resting places.
Isaiah 32:18

I waved goodbye to James and Ethan as their car rounded the corner of our country lane. The early morning light was just ascending on the new day, and it crowned the pine treetops in gold. The air was apple crisp, but I was a little heart heavy like I get when I feel both antsy about something and dumb for feeling that way. The boys were meeting a friend for a hike in the mountains, and I patted myself on the back for resisting the urge to tell them how nervous I still get about their adventuring.

Yeah, yeah, I know they're essentially grownup men. I know they're adults by law. But I also know that the rational part of their brains won't be fully formed till age twenty-five, and they're a ways off from twenty-five. Any mama of a teen will tell you that it doesn't matter what your precious darling scored on the ACT or how responsible he or she is. Any kid is susceptible to up and leaving their good judgment at home next to the extra water bottle you know they should bring but, in their words, "don't need."

Yours truly here has no desire to be attached to my sons' hips, but I do like to know if they're okay or if—in this case—they're a dinner prospect for a bear or mountain lion.

Cell phone coverage and mountains aren't exactly simpatico, so for the umpteenth time, I was forced to do what mamas of older kids or anyone separated from a loved one has been forced to do since the dawn of time: pray our guts out for God to stay glued next to our people when we can't. When we shouldn't. And, if I'm being completely honest, I was simultaneously lamenting with anyone who'd listen about my ever-growing awareness that I have no stinkin' control over anything going on in their lives.

However, this vivid lesson also showed me this: the older my kids get, the more practiced I get at dealing with said lack of control. With time, I adapt to it. With time, the growing pains of the separations aren't so acute. My mind is less likely to dwell on my kids' whereabouts and all the Big Disastrous Things that could be happening wherever they are.

And so it goes with change. The more I learn to acknowledge, accept, and adapt to it, the more I can abide in God's promise to use it for good. The more I can rest in trusting God will get me and my loved ones where we're supposed to be. Whether the change is due to a relentless difficult season or a brand-new one, I can abide in Jesus when I lean into the change he allows rather than resist it.

And we do this by walking through it with intention, staying in step with the Father rather than our own fears.

I don't always pull this off so well.

But after watching the boys leave that morning, I did pull out my little queue of short Scripture verses I have written on spiralbound notecards. Reciting them in one form or another lowers the temperature on my anxious feelings before they have the opportunity to simmer and boil over. I think of them as "breath prayers." Orthodox Christians pray something similar to the rhythm of breathing: "Lord Jesus Christ, Son of God, have mercy on me."[1]

And so it goes with change. The more I learn to acknowledge, accept, and adapt to it, the more I can abide in God's promise to use it for good.

For my own breath prayers, I recite a short Scripture, such as one of these below, as I breathe in:

"Be still, and know that I am God."[2]

"I am with you always."[3]

"For freedom Christ has set us free."[4]

Then I exhale any fears I have over the change: "Lord, I give you my fear over _____."

I do these breath prayers slowly during my morning stretches or while washing dishes, taking a shower, or driving to my daughter's tennis practice. I might take my notecards with me on walks or read a few before I go to sleep. Slowly and methodically, I breathe in his directives and breathe out the disquiet, and in doing so redirect the backward steps I've taken through that point in the day.

In the words of Elisabeth Elliot, I hang my soul on these strong pegs.[5]

I want to say that after twenty-five years as a wife, nearly twenty years as a military wife and parent, and over forty-five years as a person on this planet, I've completely reconciled my feelings about change. I want to say I've made peace with its upheaval. In truth, I can't say any of that. For heaven's sake, my baby girl just got her driver's license, so on that front I'm starting over in my recommitment to abide in Jesus. But in that is this truth: a large part of moving through a change is staying connected to Christ—abiding in him. Relating to him through breath prayers is one powerful way to keep the connection strong.

"Do not fear, only believe" (Mark 5:36).

Breathe out fear, breathe in faith.

Breathe out panic, breathe in peace.

Breathe out anxiety, breathe in affirmation.

With every next breath, abide in this God-reality: change is just God's next step to our next best thing.

Our next step is to take Jesus at his Word, believing he has not forgotten us in our life change but is working through it with every breath we take.

May we slow down, pray up, and continue to walk in anticipation rather than trepidation. May we abide in him—and abide in a quieter posture on the inside during change.

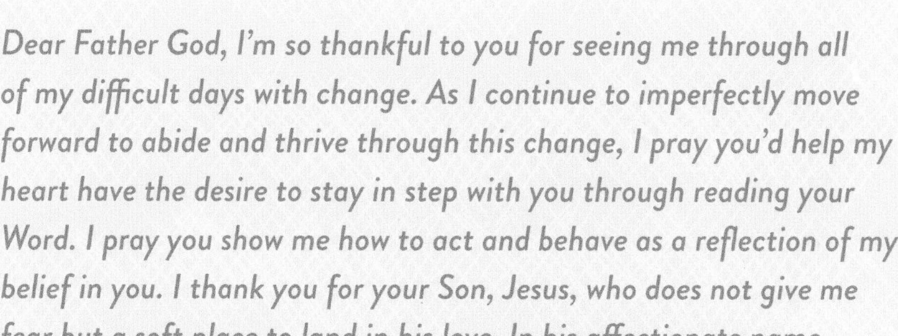

Dear Father God, I'm so thankful to you for seeing me through all of my difficult days with change. As I continue to imperfectly move forward to abide and thrive through this change, I pray you'd help my heart have the desire to stay in step with you through reading your Word. I pray you show me how to act and behave as a reflection of my belief in you. I thank you for your Son, Jesus, who does not give me fear but a soft place to land in his love. In his affectionate name I pray, amen.

"If you believe in a God who controls the big things, you have to believe in a God who controls the little things. It is we, of course, to whom things look 'little' or 'big.' Amy Carmichael wrote: 'There is no great with Thee, there is no small, For Thou art all, and fillest all in all.'" ~Elisabeth Elliot, Let Me Be a Woman

Change is just God's next step to your next best thing. Stay connected to Christ and stay connected to abiding well through change.

DAY 24

You're Strong in Scars and Stars

Then he said to Thomas, "Put your finger into my hands. Put your hand into my side. Don't be faithless any longer. Believe!"
John 20:27 TLB

The oldest of three daughters, I favor my dad in appearance. I have his wide-set eyes, which I love, and his Roman nose, which I would've been fine with him keeping. I mean, I think it looks fine on a man but isn't so flattering on a woman. However, I do enjoy pleasant scents, so I suppose it helps me breathe in my beloved citrus bliss essential oil and grapefruit-sage candle. Of course, with a menagerie of pets including two dogs, it also helps me breathe in other smells I could do without, but I digress.

From Dad I also received what is known as *pectus excavatum*, a hereditary condition passed down from his own dad. Additionally referred to as "funnel chest" or "caved-in chest," it's a congenital malformation of the chest wall resulting in a funnel-shaped depression over the lower part of the sternum. It can cause a host of problems, such as interfering with sustained exercise, recovery from respiratory infections, and carrying a pregnancy to term because of the heart's lack of capacity to handle the extra blood flow.

Thankfully, my parents took these health concerns seriously and selflessly drove me back and forth between our hometown of Ponca City, Oklahoma, and a specialist in Tulsa. My *pectus excavatum* was particularly severe, so when I was about eleven years old, the specialist suggested surgery as the best recourse. While that surgery required no small amount of recovery, I'm so thankful I had it because without it, it would've been difficult to carry my babies—let alone twins—to a healthy delivery.

That surgery happened over thirty-five years ago, and when I look at myself in the mirror, I can still see its scar stretching from under my neck to a little north of my belly button. It has faded now, and really, I almost never think about it. However, that was a whole different story in my teens and early twenties. I hated wearing bathing suits or tops that might show the scar. As is typical of that age, I was hyperaware of how I looked and assumed everyone else was just as conscious of my scar as I was. (Note to any young'un reading this: no one is looking at you with the scrutiny you think they are.) Most of the time, folks weren't dwelling on it like I thought, but I had just enough people ask about it to make me err on the side of insecurity. I was a long 'n' lanky girl who didn't fit into her skin on a good day, and I figured this scar just upped the awkward ante all the more.

I hate the way this goes—how we can read and know we're fearfully and wonderfully made but still feel like our scars testify to the opposite. We focus on our scars instead of the whole picture that is each one of us.

Change convinces us to do the same: to focus on the scars it leaves us (and maybe never get past the wounds that caused the scars in the first place) instead of focusing on the absolute wonder that is our whole selves.

Recently, I heard Pastor Brady Boyd talk about scars in a completely new way, or at least new to me. A scar becomes more powerful than the skin surrounding it because it's the body's way of saying, "I'm not letting this part of the body get hurt again." So, where the skin was damaged, it now has an extra layer of protection. Because of this, what was once a place of weakness becomes a place of strength on your body. In short, scars are God's way of taking the broken places on the body and making them places of strength.[1]

Great day, I wish teenage Kristen could've known this, but grown-up Kristen is glad to know it now. Each scar is an area of strength—a badge of honor, a sign of a battle won. A sign of love and attention. We can be proud of them, not embarrassed by them.

When we've been pushing through change for a while, can there come a point when we're proud of ourselves for making it through rather than embarrassed we had to go through it? Today, the change may cause us to feel overwhelmed, undesirable, or just plain ugly. But we want to rely on the facts of our faith, not our feelings. In light of that, the scars left by change are places of strength—they make us stronger as they grow us toward God's abundance for us.

When Thomas looked at Jesus's scars, he quit doubting and believed.[2] As we abide in Jesus, may we look at our own scars from change and believe, like Thomas, that Jesus's presence isn't going anywhere. "And he is before all things, and in him all things hold together" (Col. 1:17).

Our scars from change strengthen us from the inside out. They show the redemptive heart of God that turns something damaged into something that's powerful and protected. What was once life-diminishing is life-improving.

No matter the tilt and whirl of change in this world, we are held together because of Christ.

No matter the tilt and whirl of change in this world, we are held together because of Christ—the One who touches our scars and turns them into stars that light the way to all the ways he turns problems into praise.

And changes scars into settings of strength.

Dear Father in heaven, you know it's hard for me to see the scars brought on by change in a positive light. Help me to change my perspective so that I see them as strength, not weakness. Show me how my scars are seams of your faithfulness, because your Word says you bind up my wounds. You are in a position of power and strength that no person or circumstance can match. Help me to abide through faith that you are my strength and song. In the all-powerful name of Jesus, amen.

"My scars remind me that I did indeed survive my deepest wounds. That in itself is an accomplishment. And they bring to mind something else too. They remind me that the damage life has inflicted on me has, in many places, left me stronger and more resilient. What hurt me in the past has actually made me better equipped to face the present." ~Steve Goodier

See your scars from change as a source of strength and proof of God's faithful presence.

DAY 25

Carry Traditions to Ease Transitions

Remember these commands and cherish them. Tie them on your arms and wear them on your foreheads as a reminder. Teach them to your children. Talk about them when you are at home and when you are away, when you are resting and when you are working.

Deuteronomy 11:18–19 GNT

I'm sitting alone at the Panera off Nevada on the west side of Colorado Springs, looking out the window at piles and piles of snow. This winter has been colder than cold, and though I sit inside, I can feel the outside chill going right through my down jacket. A small party talks in the booth catty-corner to me, an older couple with a younger fellow. Soon after my squash soup is ready, the three of them stand up and exchange hugs. The young man's little girl is coloring pictures at the table next to them, and the older couple takes turns bending down to tell the child good-bye. It's the sweetest thing, and I wonder if the four of them routinely get together for dinner. Just the thought of that makes me warm up a little.

As they head out the door, I look out the window again, something I've done a lot this week. It's the anniversary of when my sweet daddy—a giant of a man with a heart as big as Texas—passed away. I think of that mentoring couple speaking into the life of that dark-haired gentleman. And then I think of my daddy, who often spoke into the lives of his three daughters, and I miss him.

Valentine's Day is next week, and I make a mental note to get the fixings for my Mema Rea's sugar cookies—a treat my dad's mama made that my kids love as much as Dad did.

Sometimes change shows up like it used to for me when our family moved every two to three years. In those days, outside change came before inside change. It was circumstantial before it was relational.

These days, change shows up more on the inside first, like a flood of memories over a loved one who's no longer with you.

Since my family and I have lived in the same town for ten years now, our transitions come more often via changing life stages than changing places. In the past two years, my twin sons bid farewell to high school as my daughter said hello to it. Our yearly school rhythm and family-home happenings look different today than they have at any other time. I find myself struggling with this change on the inside long before it shows up on the outside, such as wondering how my identity will shift when all our precious young'uns become full-fledged adults doing adulty things, like living on their own.

But whether change affects us on the inside or the outside first, we can bet it will affect us both ways eventually.

Change turns us loose in an ocean of unfamiliarity, and we can expend quite a bit of energy just staying afloat. Whether our changes rub against us from the outside or inside, we can know the Lord has a firm hand under our tired selves. And one of the ways he holds us and helps us abide within our change is providing us with recognizable landmarks to set our sights on along the way.

Traditions have become those reliable landmarks that help my family survive the wax and wane, ebb and flow of transitions. And the good thing about traditions is you can carry them all through your changing seasons and locations. For our family, traditions lasso a measure of stability and reaffirm our belonging with each other. Amid all transitions, traditions help newness still feel like home. When you're not sure where change will take you, they help you narrow your vision to doing one small thing so you can abide well in your new place.

This I know: traditions ease transitions. Because when change alters our outside environment, it's good to have regular rituals occurring inside ourselves and our families.

This I know: traditions ease transitions.

So, I make my Mema Rea's sugar cookies for Valentine's Day and in honor of my dad. I make shepherd's pie for St. Patrick's Day. May and August birthdays bring bedroom doors decorated with streamers. We make my Mema Mary's homemade Reese's bars. We visit familiar Advent books. We also make cinnamon rolls for Christmas, and they're worth scraping the sugar/cinnamon/butter concoction off the countertops and floors for the next week. We read Scripture and tell God what we're thankful for, what we're sorry for, and what we pray for. We invite Jesus into our traditions, knowing it's because of him that we have anything and everything to celebrate at all. As Paul encourages us in 2 Thessalonians 2:15, we "stand firm and hold to the traditions that you were taught by us, either by our spoken word or by our letter."

Whether daily or seasonally, we share those traditions familiar to ourselves and our family members. We can pack them up and unpack them wherever we are. And while kids grow and family stages change, most traditions are flexible enough to change with us. We may lose some or find they look different with passing time. Our schedules from one year to the next may prevent us from giving them the same attention as in years past, but that's okay. Traditions aren't straitjackets that hold us rigidly to a list of must-dos. They're flexible landmarks in our own and our family's day-to-day, year-to-year schedules and lives.

Traditions ease transitions when you and your people do what works for you, and they give everyone fresh air. They reaffirm that though difficult change will find us, we can settle into every good and perfect gift that regularly comes down from the Father of lights, who does not change.[1]

When transitions throw you for a loop, traditions help steady you. Carry a few traditions and build lasting, meaningful touchstones of familiarity within your change.

Heavenly Father, to thrive during change, I must abide in you. Please show me today how I can use traditions to ease transitions within my heart and home. I want to follow your lead and be a safehouse for my own self as well as those nearest and dearest to me. While I know you're the only one who can do that perfectly, I believe you want me to be a source of comfort to others during change. Give me wisdom as I guide my own heart and my loved ones' hearts toward the most life-giving traditions. I love you and thank you for all the gifts and traditions you've given my family and me. May I always remember to do as 2 Thessalonians 2:15 tells, to hold on to our traditions and our familial bonds. In the life-giving name of Jesus, amen.

"I realized that tradition is priceless, whether you have a small family, a large family, or no family. Tradition doesn't have to be logical; it only has to emphasize the light of Christ and his everlasting love."
~Lori Copeland

Traditions ease transitions as they steady you and return your heart and soul to a familiar, comforting environment.

DAY 26

Say Yes to the Soup

The Lord *your God is in your midst, a mighty one who will save;*
he will rejoice over you with gladness; he will quiet you by his love;
he will exult over you with loud singing.

Zephaniah 3:17

I slid into Thanksgiving 2016 with a sizable change I didn't want or ask for: a dislocated and broken elbow. What happened, you ask? Well, let's just say I drank a perfectly swirled cocktail of my own deficient depth perception and watching football from the dizzying nosebleed seats at Texas A&M's Kyle Football Field in College Station, Texas.

And just in case you're wondering, no, I hadn't indulged in any actual cocktails. Not a lick of libation. I wish I had, because then I could blame the fall on that. But no, your girl here does this kind of thing stone-cold sober.

What started out as an amazing college visit for my husband and me with our son that mid-November ended with me in the kind of pain I hadn't experienced since childbirth. In the third quarter of the football game, while our son watched the game with other students, I stood up too quickly to use the restroom and immediately lost my balance. Cue me rolling down five stadium rows and only stopping when I plowed into an unsuspecting fellow below. Great day, the mind-jarring pain in my elbow, complete with bone protruding under the skin where God never intended, was only outdone by my extreme embarrassment over the entire event.

Thankfully, many folks jumped up to help, including the fellow I'd landed on like a ton of bricks. As David held my hand, another couple of people helped me walk down what felt like a hundred thousand steps to the nearest aid station. I was then placed in an ambulance and taken to St. Joseph's Hospital in Bryan, Texas, where I had my elbow set and my arm placed in a cast before returning to our hotel room.

Let me confess something to you here: I can be a prideful gal who detests asking others for help. As in, *I hate it*. I shun the idea of being dependent on others. But a change that bends or breaks you, literally or figuratively, shows you in black-and-white contrast your very real limitations. So here I was, hammered into the humblest of states where I realized what I needed was the one thing I hated needing: help.

No, not help. HELP.

This is what I started to feel the next day as we flew back to Denver. The holiday season had just gained altitude in earnest, and here I was grounded for the foreseeable future. All the problems stood at attention.

I've barely done any shopping. How will I get it all done by Christmas?

We're hosting Thanksgiving. How can I cook such a big meal—not to mention our everyday meals—with a bum arm?

My husband's work schedule has little flexibility. How do I pick my daughter up from school and get her to her myriad of activities when I can't drive?

This broken elbow seemed to add overwhelming stress, even as I also knew it could've been so much worse.

After landing in Denver and making the hour-plus drive home, we pulled into our driveway plumb exhausted. When we hauled our tired selves into the front door, I found myself overwhelmed with the most delicious scent I'd ever met in my whole life: bacon potato soup simmering in a slow cooker.

The moment I saw the hardworking slow cooker sitting on our countertop, I started crying. Here, without my having to lift a finger, was provision. Here, without one ounce of my doing, was Love coming down in the form of my friend Aimée, who urged me to sit down and let the creamy, bacon-y goodness warm me from the inside out.

I took it as the nudge I needed to reach out further for help.

So, that's what I did. I asked my small group if we could have meals delivered. And when acquaintances, not even close friends, asked us if they could bring over a meal, I said yes instead of my knee-jerk no. I asked my visiting mother-in-law to join my husband in cooking the majority of Thanksgiving dinner. I asked my friend Allison to help me decorate for Christmas. I asked Aimée if she could pick my daughter up from school when David and the boys' schedules ran off the rails. All the help we received brought Philippians 4:19 into clear view:

> My God will liberally supply (fill until full) your every need according to His riches in glory in Christ Jesus. (AMP)

God is liberal with his care and blessings. He will fill you to the brim with everything you need, but he may ask you to settle yourself in a more humbling position first.

He may ask you to ask for help.

This change left me plumb worn out from my elbow and ego that constantly throbbed. But in the pain came the learning that it was more than okay—it was actually right—to lean on other people. It was an opportunity dropped from heaven to see people offer their best when I was at my worst. This change stripped many nonessentials from my life—namely a measure of my pride and so-called self-sufficiency—so I could see the essentials with greater clarity.

I'm not sure what measure of pride your change stripped away, but as you abide in the "new now" in front of you, heed the words of author Anjuli Paschall, detailing a time when she came face-to-face with her own limitations.

> When I got home, I asked for help, begged for it. Instead of pretending, I prayed. And lots of days my husband carried me towards it. It was a slow change—riddled with highs and lows. But here's the thing, love came to me. He came. He met me. And God will find you. Even in your fortress high fear or unbearable shame or tar-like blackness. He will come.[1]

He will come.

He will help you abide through this change—depend on it.

Dear Father God, I want to learn to abide well through this change, but it's hard to do that if I'm pridefully clinging to my own independence. Thank you for the ways you lovingly dismantle my pride, even if it's painful. Within the pain, Lord, show me today one kind of provision that surprises and delights me. Let it be a messenger of hope to my heart. Thank you for loving me through strangers and friends alike, and thank you for your Son. In his name I pray, amen.

"The benevolence of Christ leans toward kinship, where we take turns being filled with the feasts of wanting and relief."
~Shannan Martin, The Ministry of Ordinary Places

Asking for help removes the luxury of pride. During times of painful change, God will fill you to the brim with everything you need, but he may ask you to settle yourself into a more humbling position first.

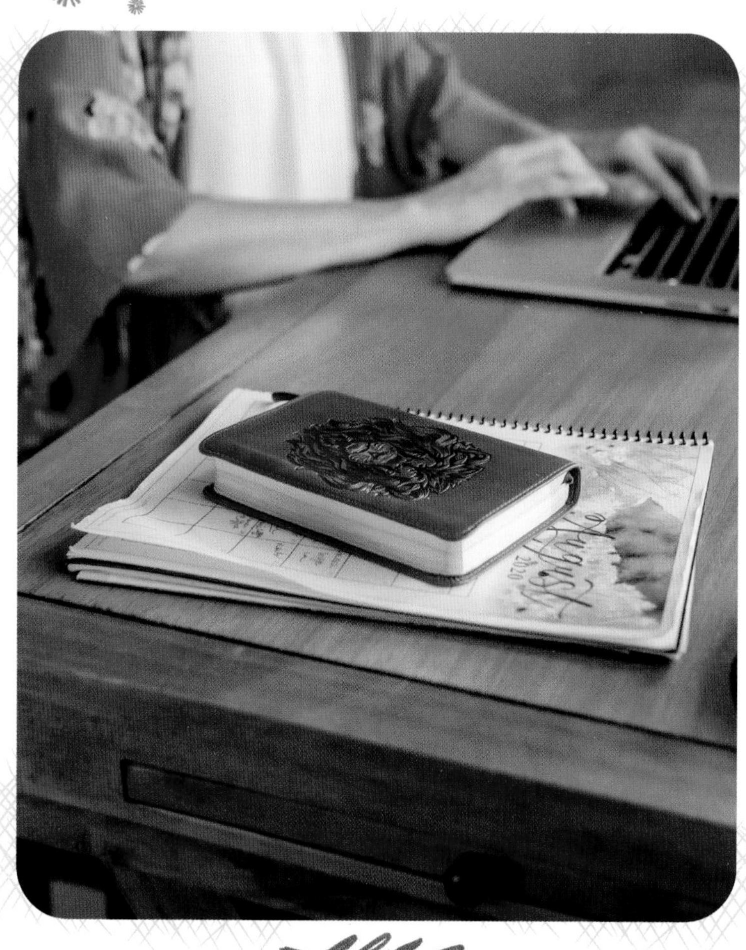
August
2020

DAY 27

Ask Different Questions

Don't bargain with God. Be direct. Ask for what you need. This is not a cat-and-mouse, hide-and-seek game we're in. If your little boy asks for a serving of fish, do you scare him with a live snake on his plate? If your little girl asks for an egg, do you trick her with a spider? As bad as you are, you wouldn't think of such a thing—you're at least decent to your own children. And don't you think the Father who conceived you in love will give the Holy Spirit when you ask him?

Luke 11:10–13 Message

As I write this today, we're under a shelter-in-place order to stay home as much as possible due to a pandemic. It's been a long several weeks, my friends. Are we on week nine or ninety-seven? I have no idea. Change sometimes happens in a moment, yes, but its repercussions can also drag on and on and *on*, causing us to question if everything from our daggum clocks to our sanity are operating as usual. Today is the first day of a new month, and I reverently turned the page on our kitchen calendar to that new month with all the grandeur of Queen Elizabeth completing an ancient ceremonial ritual.

Sometimes, we must get our fun where we can, folks.

Sometimes, we're just happy for the passage of time as we pray we're one day closer to a more hopeful future.

Last week alone about did me in. First of all, I got into a doozy of a fight with everyone under my roof. (And we all know that if one person is having trouble getting along with several other people, it's most likely that the problem is with the person—read: *me*—who is the common denominator.) Second of all, my oven door decided that a shelter-in-place order was an excellent time to refuse to close. Third, one child received devastating news, and like any self-respecting Enneagram 2, I instinctively went into overdrive thinking how I could ease his pain while simultaneously internalizing everything he was going through. None of these were huge on their own, but banded together they began stirring up my anxiety. Eventually, I gave David and the kids a temporary "*Sayonara*, dearies." I may not be able to leave the house much, but I can retreat to the bedroom for a nap.

Never underestimate the power of a good nap to reset your internal emotional clock, if only by a little.

But it's likely that when you wake up, new questions about why you must go through this whole mess will wake up too. Because while change reveals our known and unknown expectations, it also brings a truckload of questions. *Why must this change be happening? Why must I have insult added to injury? Will I be okay afterward? The calendar proves this has been catastrophically long—will it ever end?*

Well, as Christians we can be thankful that asking all the questions is always a wise move. As I just learned while working through Beth Moore's Bible study, *The Quest*,[1] the Bible itself holds almost 3,300 God-breathed questions.[2] Many of them are asked sideways, that is person-to-person, person-to-angel, Jesus-to-person, and other "lateral" options. But many of them are asked vertically too, as in God-to-person or person-to-God. Asking God questions like those above is certainly encouraged. I also wonder if we would do ourselves a favor by not letting those questions be the beginning and end of our conversations. Instead, what if we follow up our raw and real questions with more raw and real questions that encourage a shift in perspective?

What if we lament and question the *outcome* of a change but also ask questions that invite God to show us the *purpose* within each change?

So, while we may begin with "Why did I have to lose that job?" we can follow up with "What better job might you, Lord, have in mind for me?"

We may cry out, "Why did he leave me?" but we can also beg for an answer to "In what redemptive way will your goodness show up for me?"

We may lament, "Why did I have to lose this loved one?" but we can also raise the question "Can you show me, Lord, that my loss matters and her life mattered?"

Instead of only asking, "Why did I have to get so sick?" we can follow that with "Can you show me and my loved ones, God, how you bring out the best from the worst of circumstances?"

These follow-up questions give us the ability to recalibrate our hearts and shift our perspective, something God used questions for in the Bible too.[3]

Our problem, I believe, is that when we hear the unproductive questions that Satan or a wayward person asks us, we begin to question God rather than the enemy.

> Now the serpent was more crafty than any other beast of the field that the LORD God had made. He said to the woman, "Did God actually say, 'You shall not eat of any tree in the garden'?" (Gen. 3:1)

Satan asks, "Did God really say?" And like Eve, we water and tend to this seed of suggestion by believing the change is here because God is holding out on us. See the lie for what it is, dear one. We are not the exception to God's rule of faithfulness and love. If a change is in our life, then let us abide in the truth that God has only good intentions for it.

While I pondered this, my MacGyver husband figured out a way to keep the oven door where it's supposed to be so it can do what it's supposed to do. Sure, it currently looks like something the Clampetts might've jerry-rigged, but it works—glory be! I received forgiveness from my people for the 232nd time since the quarantine started. Our child's disappointment still hurts somethin' fierce, and there's only more questions than answers at this point in time. So, instead of sitting in that anxiety, I ask, "God, what redemptive, wrong-made-right work are you up to during this change?"

If a change is in our life, then let us abide in the truth that God has only good intentions for it.

And I abide in knowing this: all our questions will one day be answered through God's gracious plans stretching from this moment to the foreseeable—and unforeseeable—future.

Dear Father in heaven, you know how I can resemble a runaway train with all my questions that take me further and further from your heart. Please encourage me to ask you the natural, heart-wrenching questions because you're my safest place to do so. Also, please encourage me to not stop there—to ride the tide of faith and ask you those perspective-shifting follow-up questions too. Thank you that you hear and are interested in every one of my questions, Lord. In the name of Jesus, whose life answers every important question, amen.

"It's OK to ask, 'Where are you?' He won't shame you; he'll show you. He was always there, always watching, always with you and for you and carrying you through." ~Kaitlyn Bouchillon

While it's okay to question the outcome of a change, you also want to ask God to show you the purpose within each change.

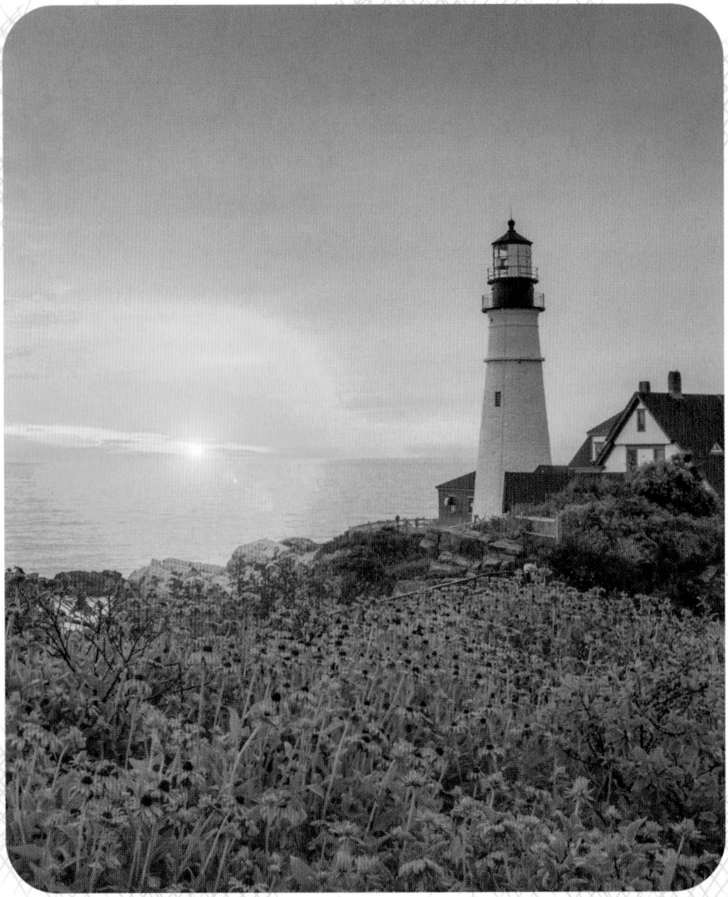

DAY 28

Let Life's Nor'easters Launch You Forward

Jesus answered him, "What I am doing you do not understand now, but afterward you will understand."

John 13:7

If I asked you to name a calendar year that was particularly hard for you, I bet you could name it (snaps fingers) like that. While 2020 will go down as one of those for more of us than not, I'll tell you another one of mine: 2018. I won't relay all the gory details, but suffice to say it sucked. By the time Christmas came to 2018, I was ready to use my size-11 feet to kick the whole more-bitter-than-sweet year out the front door and into oblivion. Some of our changes were wanted and right on schedule—a celebratory part of our family's story, like our sons graduating from high school. That change may have been emotionally hard, but it was as things were supposed to be. Difficult, but not unwanted. The majority of our changes were not wanted or appreciated—no, ma'am. Several knocked us clean over, like a fast-moving storm at sea slamming into us as we sat in a pontoon boat.

That year is receding in the distance now, but I can still vividly recall the nausea and motion sickness from it that kept us shaken and stirred and hugging the closest facilities.

I've never experienced a nor'easter, a storm that typically brings strong winds, heavy precipitation, rough seas, and coastal flooding to the northeast region of the United States. I mean, your girl here gets seasick at the mere mention of a boat ride, so I can't imagine what fun this kind of storm would be.

However, you can bet I've experienced a nor'easter figuratively. You know of what I speak. You get one change sent your way, and you're holding on just fine. But then another change smacks right into you, and it's just too much. The sudden job loss *and* the secret discovered. The out-of-the-blue diagnosis *and* a child's debilitating struggle. The breakdown of that relationship *and* the breakdown of the family car. The private heartbreak *and* the public scrutiny. It's all too much for this day, this season, this year. You keep moving one foot in front of the other in order to do the next small thing—pack the school lunch, drive to soccer practice, pay the electric bill. But every once in a while, you get lost staring out the window.

You get lost wishing the view in front of you didn't plumb shatter your heart.

My friend Cheryl's "nor'easter" came in 2019. Within weeks of sending their youngest to college, her husband found out he was headed overseas for a short-notice deployment. Facing an empty nest was one thing, but dealing with an unforeseen deployment and a short supply of time with her husband beforehand on top of an empty nest? That's a lot on a heart. If only the sadness and loneliness it brought could be in short supply too.

Job from the Old Testament knew no small amount of sadness, as he faced a figurative nor'easter like few others. Tragedy after tragedy befell him, including the loss of all his children, servants, and livestock. When he was in the middle of receiving largely unhelpful counsel from friends, Job said out loud, "Would he contend with me in the greatness of his power? No; he would pay attention to me" (Job 23:6).

I find comfort that in the middle of his own loss, Job named the fact that God paid attention to the losses he endured. God wasn't uninterested or removed from Job's pain. He wasn't aloof and above it all. He cared.

It makes me ask myself, In my own nor'easter of change, as I let my own words, thoughts, and feelings tumble outward, do I pay attention to the unchanging, full-on attention God gives me? Pain is never proof that God isn't paying attention. Pain is proof that God's heart breaks right alongside us—and his presence goes with us.

Pain is never proof that God isn't paying attention. Pain is proof that God's heart breaks right alongside us—and his presence goes with us.

Recently, I read that psychologists are spending more and more time studying what's known as post-traumatic growth, as "surviving hard periods in life can often make us more focused, more compassionate, more spiritual, and more aware of our own strengths and possibilities."[1] When God permits the nor'easters of change to drench us, I wonder if these good things—compassion, spiritual strengths, and more focused attention—are what he sees that need to rise to the surface and wash onto the shore of our lives.

When change after change in the form of storm after storm comes, it can be hard to keep abiding in Jesus. It's tempting to quit by giving in to the panic and simmering fear. But that's when we need to know that while our storms saturate us, we have a Parent who is looking with the long view of love. It's also important to remember that the downtimes have the potential to propel us forward in a way we wouldn't have been otherwise. Job 42:10 says, "And the Lord restored the fortunes of Job, when he had prayed for his friends." Job allowed his loss to move him forward in empathy. And out of that empathy, he prayed for his friends as a way of doing something for others.

Sometimes we go through great change so God can use us to greatly change someone else's life for the better.

As my pastor, Mark Bates, teaches, God isn't *almost* sovereign, nor is his influence limited. He is sovereign, period. He influences all the things in our life all the time for our good always. With this promise in our pocket, we can see our own nor'easters as places to grow and mature as we persevere. They're our opportunities to stand as a lighthouse on the shore, a fixed place for others to look to as a source of hope when storms beat and batter.

Then, one day, we can look back at the hardest of years and see how maybe, just maybe, they propelled us forward into the best of years.

Dear God, help me remember that though I am uncomfortable, even miserable, today, I can be stronger and more resilient tomorrow. Propel me forward through this change, Lord. Remind me how I can use it to help others and be a lighthouse on the shore that points to you. Give me peace during my present circumstances and reassurances for the future that you are in the boat with me. Thank you for your Son, Jesus, who fulfilled every desire we could ever want or need by his work on the cross. In his saving name, amen.

"I have learned to kiss the wave that throws me against the Rock of Ages." ~Charles Spurgeon

When the nor'easters of life come, God hasn't forgotten you. He's paying attention to you. See what goodness the Lord will wash onto the shores through these storms, and see how your great change could be an opportunity to greatly change someone else's life for the better.

DAY 29

When You're in a Tight Space, Get Down Low

Thank God no matter what happens. This is the way God wants you who belong to Christ Jesus to live.

1 Thessalonians 5:18 Message

When our precious children were knee-high to a grasshopper, my husband traveled all the ever-lovin' time for work. The nature of his business meant he usually worked at military bases and therefore stayed in base lodging of one kind or another. If there was no on-base lodging available, he stayed in a Holiday Inn or something else of the simple variety—no fuss, no frills, no fancy. The hotels were the kind where Eleanor Shellstrop from *The Good Place* would've hollered, "Ya basic!"

When David returned home from one of these work trips (usually in the evening, just in time to rile the kids up before bedtime, but I digress), he often brought each child a present, and the present was always the same: either a notepad or a pen from the hotel room. And let me tell you, each and every time, the kids acted like their dad had presented them with the Hope Diamond. Or maybe a bin of LEGOs, as that would've held more value in their wee-watt minds. They would squeal and squeeze his neck and run off to employ that notepad or pen with utmost efficiency. They took no small amount of pride in their amassed collection of paper with "Nellis Air Force Base" written across the top or a pen with "Fairfield Inn" emblazoned on the side. There's no happy like the happy that comes from free writing supplies, I suppose.

Like most kids, mine could also find joy in rocks, roly polies, and magic "potions" comprised of leaves and tree berries from around the neighborhood. These simple front yard gems provided as much happiness as their bikes or their Hot Wheels cars. You and I probably felt the same when we were little and a little wild too.

But somewhere along the way, we grown-ups easily become jaded or cynical or just plain blind to the simple things. We stop getting down low to the ground to see the glory that is in the small and unassuming. And I'm as bad as anyone. I have to sometimes check my Big Fat Entitlement attitude because the feeling that rises up when, for example, my favorite coffee shop tells me they're out of chai ain't pretty.

It ain't pretty at all.

But when I have an active awareness of abiding well through change, I mimic our young'uns and figuratively get low to the ground. I'm not as apt to look so far ahead that all I see are impossible obstacles and problems. Instead, I see a host of gifts to be thankful for.

But I can't be thankful for something if I don't even see it in the first place.

It's easier to do this on a more ideal morning with a chai latte in one hand and nothing in front of me but my own agenda and plans. However, it's harder during those many times change has put me in such a tight space that it feels virtually impossible to name the favorable. I'm too busy trying not to hyperventilate to be thankful for the blue sky or the singing birds or the way the sun moves through the pine trees. Besides, it's too dark to see any of those things anyway.

But what if those tight spaces hold as many good things as the wide-open spaces?

Moses spent quite a bit of time with God, but as detailed in Exodus 33, he didn't just want to spend time with God. He wanted to *see* God. Because don't we all want to eventually lay eyes on the one whom we deeply love?

So, Moses, with a bit of brazen fortitude, asked God to show him his glory. He wanted to experience God in a new, deeper way. He wanted to be as close to God as possible.[1] God granted Moses his request with one caveat: knowing a straight-on view of God would be too much for Moses to take in, he told Moses he'd see his glory from behind. To protect him, God placed Moses in the crevice of a rock and covered him with his hand while passing by.

I am not unfamiliar with the idea that says to know God's glory, we are sometimes asked to sit in tight places. But as I read those verses from Exodus, what I uncover is this: When change puts me in tight places, is it especially dark because God's hand is covering and protecting me too? Can I believe it's dark because of mercy and protection rather than abandonment?

> The Lord granted that which would abundantly satisfy. God's goodness is his glory; and he will have us to know him by the glory of his mercy, more than by the glory of his majesty. Upon the rock there was a fit place for Moses to view the goodness and glory of God.[2]

Perhaps our own dark, tight spaces are a fit place to see the goodness and glory of God too. And seeing it can look like naming it and being thankful for it.

God moves from his own wisdom, not ours. In seasons of change, the dark may linger far longer than we expected it to. But there is something kind and hopeful about knowing that the darkness, like a winter that outstays its welcome, still lingers from God's wisdom and goodness. And we will see his goodness when we go looking for it. Our own personal gratitude list, however we choose to keep it, can be one powerful way to see a measure of God's protection within our pressed-in places.

When change puts me in tight places, is it especially dark because God's hand is covering and protecting me too?

So, make a list of what you're thankful for, just whisper it in the carpool line, or name it while you're strolling down aisle 8 of the grocery store. "Give thanks in all circumstances; for this is the will of God in Christ Jesus for you" (1 Thess. 5:18).

Give thanks in all—in times of calm and times of change.

Give thanks . . . and abide in him.

Dear Father God, I get so scared when I sit in a tight space. Right now, even breathing feels nearly impossible. Help me see my own tight space as a fit place for your mercy and protection. Help me to abide in this truth by being thankful for all you give all the time—because you're good all the time. Thank you for your Son, Jesus, who is with us through every tight space and every changing place. In his generous name, amen.

"When life hits you hard, just know that is when God is fighting for you the hardest." ~Salena Duffy

A tight place can be a fit place to see God's goodness. It may be dark, but not from abandonment. Practicing gratitude in your own tight space shows you all the ways God's mercy and protection are ever-present.

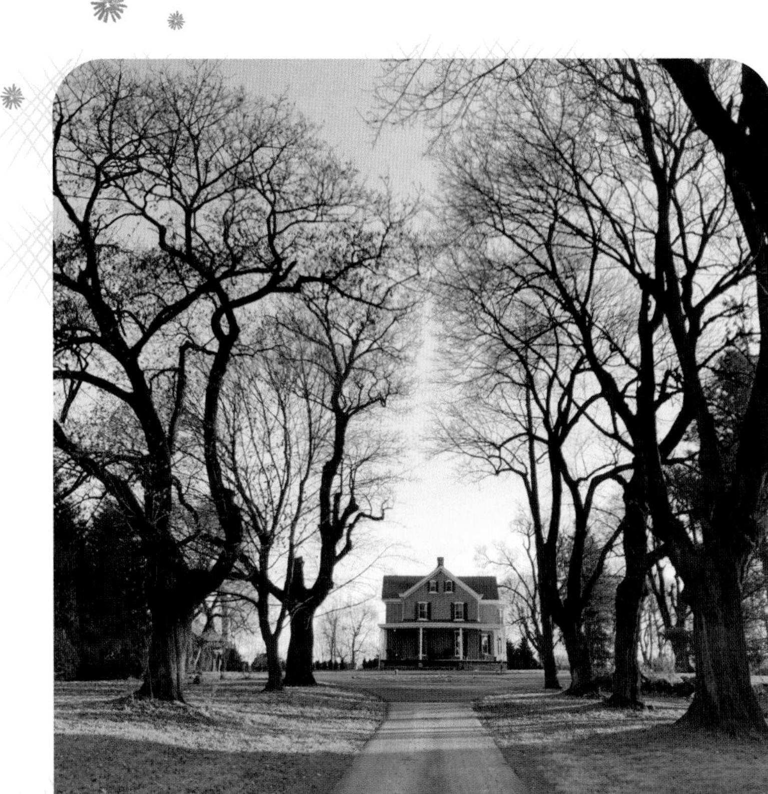

DAY 30

Believe in Expiration Dates

When Jesus had received the sour wine, he said, "It is finished," and he bowed his head and gave up his spirit.

John 19:30

Mema Rea passed down to me, alongside her Mile-High Strawberry Pie recipe and an affinity for *My Fair Lady*, a love for biographies. One of the things I remember her reading most was biographies of first ladies—those she loved and those she . . . didn't.

So, I always feel a little closer to my mema when I read about a first lady. Not only that, but I've discovered there's much to be learned from these women who endured change on a level that few can comprehend. Many were regular people who, like my mema, came from humble beginnings. However modest or majestic their roots, God's plans propelled them in a direction where they dealt with drastic change in full view of the public. As I have learned from my own older family members how to abide through change, I can also learn from many of these women, whatever their political affiliation. I can see aspects of myself through the lens of their changing circumstances and let them teach me how to handle—and how not to handle—my own change.

One former first lady I find courageous is Betty Ford. First lady from 1974 to 1977, Betty first set foot in the White House as its resident after President Nixon's resignation. Only a few short weeks after she became first lady, a routine mammogram revealed Betty had a lump in her breast. So, at the end of a jam-packed day that included a groundbreaking ceremony, a speech on behalf of the Salvation Army, and a White House tour to former first lady Lady Bird Johnson and her daughters, Betty left for Bethesda Naval Hospital for her surgery.

In the 1970s, cancer was largely called "the 'C' word," as if saying *cancer* made it contagious. Even if cancer itself was discussed, almost no one said the word *breast* in conversation.[1] Betty, knowing the number of women dying from cancer each year, told her staffers to be completely honest to the general public about what she was undergoing at the hospital. In other words, none of this "general procedure" verbiage. Given the time and culture surrounding cancer, this was a monumentally big deal.

When surgery revealed a malignant tumor, Betty underwent a total mastectomy, which wasn't unusual at that time. However, what was uncommon *and* remarkable was the way she shared her diagnosis with the American public through televised press conferences.[2] After her mastectomy, Betty urged other women confronting breast cancer to have the surgery "as quickly as possible."[3] She spoke out too about the importance of early detection. While her recovery wasn't easy, she didn't shy away from that part of her story. She bravely and repeatedly addressed her private experiences in a very public way, and this encouraged and helped thousands.

Betty went on to receive over fifty thousand letters from women crediting her with saving their lives as her openness and vulnerability encouraged them to seek their own medical treatment.[4]

Later in life, Betty approached her addiction to alcohol and pain pills with the same candor and honesty. As a way to encourage others to do the same, she opened the world-famous Betty Ford Center so more people could face their addiction struggles too.

I don't know how much Betty's faith informed her everyday life, but it seems that when it comes to difficult change, this former first lady could've given a master class in the art of abiding well through it. She faced it as it was, not what she wished it was. Betty, whose life had known crisis after crisis since childhood, approached each one with matter-of-fact truthfulness. Speaking of her cancer diagnosis, she wrote, "This is one more crisis, and it will pass."[5]

Betty approached each one with a help plus hope mentality: get the help you need to face it head-on and grasp the hope that it won't last forever.

I think of those words "This too shall pass," which my mom used to say after one of her three daughters had some kind of crisis, big or small. She was right too. Jesus said something similar when he uttered the phrase "It is finished," right before he breathed his last on the cross.[6] In Greek, that word translated "finished" is *tetelestai*. Taken literally, it means ended, accomplished, paid, and complete.[7] Jesus's death on the cross tells us that our own suffering will end too. Jesus's resurrection says we can always, always land on hope raising itself up in the end.

We can abide well through change when we remember every pain and struggle from change has an expiration date, and we can believe this because God has gotten us through 100 percent of every change we've ever faced. He'll get us through this one too.

God has gotten us through 100 percent of every change we've ever faced. He'll get us through this one too.

There's power in calling the change what it is: another crisis that will, like all the rest, eventually pass.

Yes, abiding well through difficult change is no summer picnic. But that change is part of how God is weaving your own story into a legacy of hope . . . and a biography of grace.

Dear faithful Father, I wholeheartedly thank you for all the ways you've taken care of me through past crises. As you've seen me through troubling change before, I know you will see me through it now. You will see to it that this change passes, leaving me way past where I am today—leaving me as a refined, strengthened, and more whole person who can tell of your faithfulness and trust to others. Lord, build perseverance inside me as you help me abide through this change by holding on to a help plus hope mindset. I love you.
In Jesus's steadfast name, amen.

"Either Jesus Christ is a deceiver . . . or some extraordinary thing happens to a man who holds on to the love of God when the odds are against God's character. Logic is silenced in the face of every one of these things. Only one thing can account for it—the love of God in Christ. 'Out of the wreck I rise' every time."
~*Oswald Chambers,* My Utmost for His Highest

One day you will see the other side of this change. But for today, hold on to a help plus hope mindset. When you do, you will be able to share about God's faithfulness with others.

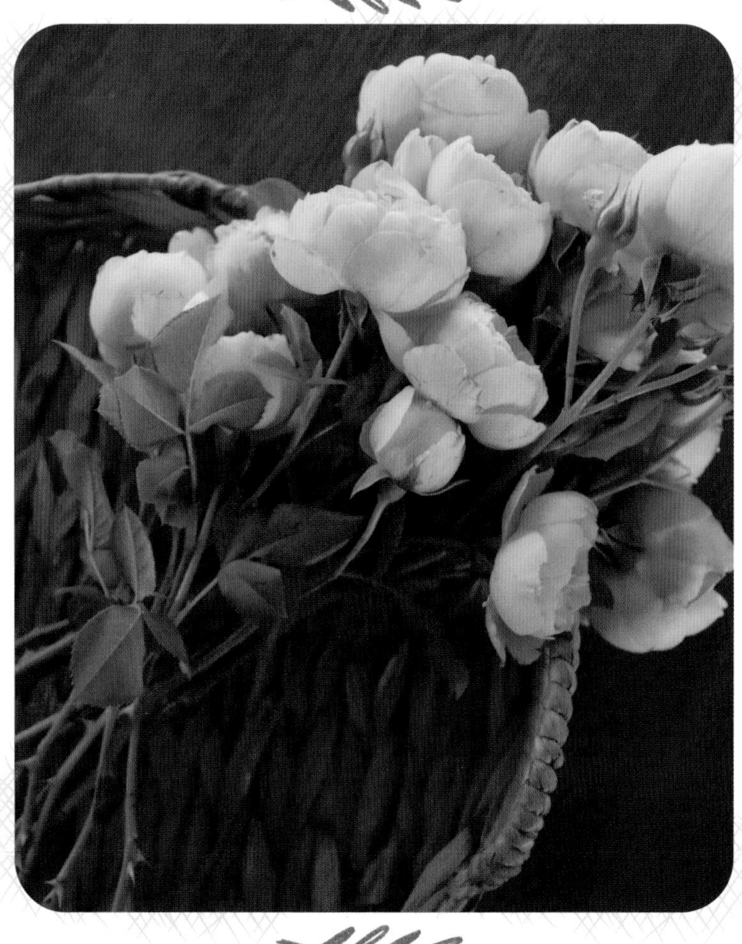

DAY 31

What the Jonas Brothers and the Rest of Us Have in Common

I am the vine; you are the branches. Whoever abides in me and I in him, he it is that bears much fruit, for apart from me you can do nothing.

John 15:5

When you have a sixteen-year-old daughter who loves herself some Jonas Brothers, you're treated to the band's music reverberating on repeat all about the house. *A lot*. To be honest, yours truly here doesn't really mind it. I kind of like their music too, in spite of the fact that I'm decades outside their target audience. Their tunes are generally catchy and lighthearted, a nice escape from a world full of change that often feels anything but. That's probably why I willingly treated Faith to their Denver concert for her birthday and subsequently sacrificed my hearing to the wild screams of eighteen thousand of our closest friends for three straight hours.

Because I'm endlessly fascinated with behind-the-scenes stories, I also don't mind watching anything "JoBros" related with Faith, like their documentary or their concert event. I enjoy hearing about their familial relationships, especially the brothers' reflections on why they broke up their band for a few years and why they got back together.

In their "Happiness Continues" feature on Amazon Prime, each brother gives a short, compelling reflection about why the breakup needed to happen.

> Kevin: "The breakup needed to happen so we could find ourselves as individuals . . . so we could come back and do this better."
>
> Nick: "When we got back together it was about actually going in and reopening some of those wounds to properly heal them. Because you can't just slap another Band-Aid on it. You have to get in and see what's really there."
>
> Joe: "We really healed, and we really have mended a broken relationship. And now we're better than we've ever been."[1]

I wasn't familiar with the Jonas Brothers as a band before their breakup, but their present comments imply that each brother is able to see the positive that followed the brokenness and separation from their changed relationship. I'm not sure if they'd word this as I'm about to here, but perhaps they can look upon their breakup as a band, and more importantly as three close brothers, and see it as an intense season of pruning that needed to happen.

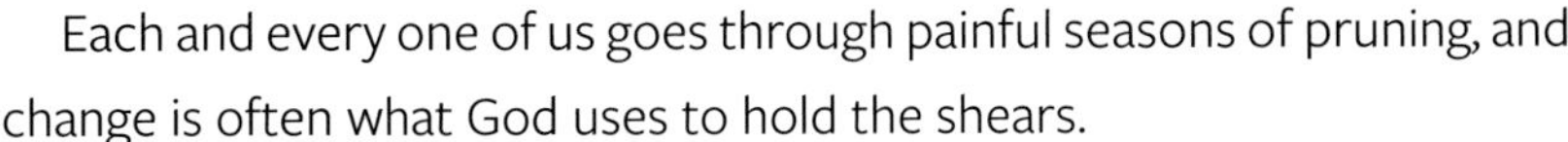

Each and every one of us goes through painful seasons of pruning, and change is often what God uses to hold the shears.

I'm a fledgling gardener on a good day, but I've always found the concept of pruning flowers fascinating. Have you ever seen a gardener really go after an established but unruly rosebush in early spring? He or she knows that to get the most blooms, one-third to one-half of the rosebush has to be removed. This seems terribly counterintuitive, that what eventually brings flourishing blooms to the rosebush first looks more like plant shrapnel lying all over kingdom come. It turns out that what looks like destruction is totally necessary, because pruning allows for increased air circulation that keeps the plant from becoming a tangled mess. Pruning also removes dead or damaged wood. And since the best flowers often sprout and multiply on new growth, pruning enables gardeners to shape their bushes in a way that best encourages the growth of flowering wood.[2]

The Gardener uses change to bring success—even though it might first look like failure.

The Gardener uses change to bring success—even though it might first look like failure.

The Gardener strips away what isn't necessary—to bring abundance in extraordinary fashion.

Jesus tells us that he is the Vine, and his Father is the Gardener. Jesus says, "Every branch in me that does not bear fruit he takes away, and every branch that does bear fruit he prunes, that it may bear more fruit" (John 15:2).

He takes away to give more.

There's no way to sugarcoat that pruning is undoubtedly unpleasant—and sometimes traumatic. But we don't need to fret that pruning means our situation is unfixable or we've messed up beyond repair. It means God sees the potential within the pain—and he will use this period to bring about maximum potential. He will use this season to mold and pattern you and me into something new and promising.

He will use it to bring about redemptive blooms.

In the meantime, what do you do while you wait through the change? You abide in Jesus. That is your only assignment as you stay connected to the Vine. Abide in Jesus. Spend time with him through reading Scripture and praying. Keep a dialogue with him about how you're really doing. Ask him all your questions. Bring a new tradition into your life and home that provides a landmark of stability and points an arrow to him. Name the gifts God gives you each day. In the words of writer Shelly Miller, look for the "windfall of God's abundance" arriving when you don't expect it.[3] He's still here, giving you good things all the time because God is good all the time.

And then one day, you'll notice you're not so apt to let that anxiety be what shows up first because you find yourself holding on to Jesus instead of the nervous feelings. You sense this message in your spirit: *this is what it looks like to bloom within change, because panic and fear don't get the final say.*

The new song in your soul does.

I'll let you decide if that song you sing is by the Jonas Brothers or someone else.

Heavenly Father, thank you that you do not leave us unto ourselves. Thank you that you love us enough to improve, strengthen, mold, and pattern us. Thank you that if you allow change to prune away something in our lives, you mean to allow bigger, better blooms to stand in its place. Help me to persevere with patience during this painful season. When my season of pruning feels like it may kill me, give me a sight of your redemptive power. I know you bring all change together for good—help me see and know it. In the ever-abiding name of Jesus, amen.

"Let's trust the Master Gardener who cares deeply about each one of us and also sees the big picture of His garden."
~Dorina Lazo Gilmore-Young

Pruning often comes by way of change, but that's not a bad thing. Pruning is a necessary means of setting us up for incredible success. While we wait for the blooms to show themselves, we abide in Jesus.

Conclusion

JUST A LITTLE NOTE

The screaming, earsplitting sounds from the house alarm jolted me awake from my sleep on a freezing Ohio night. I threw off the covers, jumped out of bed, and flew down the stairs toward the entryway wall that held the alarm console. As I frantically punched buttons, my heart pounded so loudly it took me a few seconds to decide if the alarm had actually turned off. Finally, my brain registered silence.

Miraculously, my young kids appeared to have slept right through it.

The alarm had accidentally gone off before, and I realized I'd assumed this middle-of-the-night incident was also an accident. But as I willed my heartbeat to return to some semblance of normal, I shocked myself wide-awake with one terrible thought: *Did the alarm go off this time because someone else was in the house?* Did a burglar hightail it out of there, or was he hiding behind my couch? Just as I was imagining what might happen next, my phone rang. I ran to answer it, noticing the clock read 3:12 AM.

I picked up the phone and was relieved to hear my husband's voice on the other end. He had traveled to Hawaii for work, and through a series of events I still don't quite get, the alarm company had called him when it went off instead of the police. David's voice reassured me that it appeared the problem was with one of the basement windows. "Go downstairs and see if the sensor came off, honey. I'm sure that's all that happened."

I responded with no small amount of incredulousness, "Well, all that may be good and true, but what if you're wrong? What if a killer is hiding behind Faith's play kitchen down there? What'll I do then? Shouldn't I call the police?" He told me that he had reattached that exact sensor a while back, so it had likely come loose again. "Go ahead," he encouraged. "I'll stay with you on the phone while you check it out." *A lot of good that'll do me from Hawaii*, I thought to myself. But as I descended the stairs to the basement, the rational part of me began to take over and see that he was probably right.

Sure enough, as I turned on the lights and walked toward the window, I saw the sensor lying on the windowsill. The whole shebang had been a false alarm.

Thank you, Jesus.

Thinking back on that incident reminds me that every time change comes, it will do its best to make us think it's a five-alarm fire. It's the burglar in your house stealing your peace. Sometimes it may very well be. But often it's just a lot of scary noise. No matter its scope, whether slight or serious, God will use it to help us tend to things. He will use it to help fix what's broken, to grow us toward a better place than we are in right now.

A while ago, my pastor, Mark Bates, told a story about the process Mama Eagle goes through to build a nest.[1] She gathers thorns and brambles for the base of the nest and adds bits of feathers, grass, and other softer materials on top. The baby chicks enjoy the downy, cozy nest for some time, but once they reach a certain age, Mama Eagle begins to pick out the soft parts until the nest isn't quite the comfortable haven it once was. Bit by bit, the nest becomes more pokey and painful. Mama Eagle doesn't do this to be unkind or harsh to her babies. Rather, she does it as an act of love and care. She does it with the view of nest-to-ground in mind. Mama Eagle knows that relying on comfortable surroundings could lead her offspring to a failure to launch, and a failure to launch means a failure to live and thrive—a failure to fly.

Changing the nest produces pain, yes. But it also gives way to freedom for the young birds.

Change does this for you and me too. We just have to be willing to take that first step out of our nest, which is believing this change isn't a life hindrance but a life occurrence that is a stepping-stone to God's best for us. When we do this, we can

Acknowledge the difficult losses change brings.
Accept God's promises are believable and his presence is unchangeable.
Adapt our hearts to be flexible because God's plans are purposeful.
Abide in Jesus by leaning into the change he allows.

We can begin to feel different about change on the inside, so we can then live differently on the outside. We can be a light for someone else who could benefit from the uncomfortable growth change has given us, someone who could use a positive change in their life too.

We all need reassurances that we can make it through change; we need truth spoken in a way that we can receive. I hope this book has served as a tool that does just that. I hope every day's reading has pointed to this singular message: you have everything you need to handle change because you have everything you need in Christ.

Thanks for coming alongside me here, dear reader. You've been a gift to me, as I hope these words here have been to you. I pray for God's favor on you and your family as you acknowledge, accept, adapt, and abide through this change. Today, and every day that difficult change finds you, may God grant you a more hopeful vision of your future.

You're wildly beloved.

Love,

Kristen

PS: To stay in touch with me, visit my website, www.kristenstrong.com, or find me on Instagram @kristenstrong and @girlmeetschange.

Notes

Day 1 Simmer Down, Anxiety

1. Matthew 28:20.

Day 2 Abundance Is Coming

1. As commented in Kristen Strong, "Three Reasons Your Mess Makes You a Great Mama," (in)courage, February 9, 2019, https://www.incourage.me/2019/02/three-reasons-your-mess-makes-you-a-great-mama.html#comment-246342.

Day 4 Reject the Committee of Internal Critics

1. 2 Timothy 1:7.
2. John 10:10.
3. Oswald Chambers, *My Utmost for His Highest* (Uhrichsville, OH: Barbour, 1963), May 19.

Day 5 First, Go.

1. John Piper, "The Covenant of Abraham," Desiring God, October 18, 1981, https://www.desiringgod.org/messages/the-covenant-of-abraham.

Day 6 Look for the Signs

1. Psalm 27:13 NIV.

Day 8 Remember the Relationship

1. "Man vs. Wild: A Dodgy Situation [featuring Jake Gyllenhaal]," YouTube video, 1:53, posted by Discovery, July 6, 2011, https://www.youtube.com/watch?v=fGloGR2H5yY.

2. "Courteney Cox Abseils Off the Edge of a Cliff | Running Wild with Bear Grylls," YouTube video, 2:19, posted by Discovery UK, September 2, 2016, https://www.youtube.com/watch?v=M40iW7Aw9gs.

3. Psalm 18:29.

4. Isaiah 40:4–5.

5. Ruth Chou Simons, Instagram caption, January 27, 2020, https://www.instagram.com/p/B708z5-AKtV/.

Day 10 When All You See Are Bugs, Look Again

1. Ann Voskamp, *The Greatest Gift: Unwrapping the Full Love Story of Christmas* (Wheaton, IL: Tyndale, 2013), 125–26.

Day 11 Sit and Support

1. Kate Andersen Brower, *First Women: The Grace and Power of America's Modern First Ladies* (New York: HarperCollins, 2017), 20.

2. Matthew 28:20.

3. Matthew 11:28.

4. John 16:33.

Day 13 Stay on the Track

1. Ann Donegan Johnson, *The Value of Helping: The Story of Harriet Tubman* (La Jolla, CA: Value Communications, Inc., 1979), 63.

2. @historycoolkids, Instagram caption, June 4, 2020, https://www.instagram.com/p/CBAMommDjvm/.

3. Johnson, *Value of Helping*, 63.

4. @historycoolkids, Instagram caption.

5. "Harriet Tubman Biography," *Biography*, accessed October 14, 2020, https://www.biography.com/activist/harriet-tubman.

6. "Harriet Tubman Biography."

7. @historycoolkids, Instagram caption.

8. "Harry Tubman Quotes," Goodreads, accessed October 14, 2020, https://www.goodreads.com/author/quotes/59710.Harriet_Tubman.

9. "Harry Tubman Quotes."

10. Ellie Claire, *Hello God . . . It's Me: A 365 Day Devotional Journal* (New York: Ellie Claire Gifts, 2016), March 12.

Day 14 Love First, Know Second

1. Max Lucado, @Max Lucado, Instagram caption, June 25, 2020, https://www.instagram.com/p/CB3HOK7gBKF/?hl=en.

Day 15 When Change Falls Darkest, Truth Blazes Brightest

1. Genesis 1:3.
2. Emily Maust Wood, "20 Influential Quotes by Dietrich Bonhoeffer," Crosswalk.com, November 23, 2015, https://www.crosswalk.com/faith/spiritual-life/inspiring-quotes/20-influential-quotes-by-dietrich-bonhoeffer.html.

Day 16 Reach Further

1. Erin Moon, *Every Broken Thing: A Lent & Holy Week Guide to Answering Ecclesiastes* (self-published, 2020), 37.

Day 20 Consider God's Redirection

1. "The Sound of Music Reunion," YouTube video, 43:02, posted by skyMTV, October 30, 2017, https://www.youtube.com/watch?v=pg0ex72yHi4.
2. "When the Lord Closes a Door," YouTube video, 0:39, posted by David Elder, July 20, 2017, https://www.youtube.com/watch?v=DNmp5hZBmQ4.

Day 22 Failure Can't Knock You Off Course

1. Chris Barton, *Whoosh! Lonnie Johnson's Super-Soaking Stream of Inventions* (Watertown, MA: Charlesbridge, 2016), 10.
2. "Lonnie G. Johnson Biography," Biography, July 1, 2020, https://www.biography.com/inventor/lonnie-g-johnson.
3. Barton, *Whoosh!*, 14.
4. Barton, *Whoosh!*, 18.
5. "Lonnie G. Johnson Biography."

Day 23 Lean into Breath Prayers

1. Elisabeth Elliot, *Let Me Be a Woman* (Wheaton, IL: Tyndale, 1976), 15.
2. Psalm 46:10.
3. Matthew 28:20.
4. Galatians 5:1.
5. Elliot, *Let Me Be a Woman*, 15.

Day 24 You're Strong in Scars and Stars

1. Barbara Lowe, "Podcast 63: The New Possibilities for Women with Pastor Brady Boyd," *Dr. Barbara Whole Self Whole Life* (podcast), January 22, 2020, 8:30 mark, https://drbarbaralowe.com/ep-63/.
2. John 20:24–27.

Day 25 Carry Traditions to Ease Transitions

1. James 1:17.

Day 26 Say Yes to the Soup

1. Anjuli Paschall, @Anjuli Paschall, Instagram caption, February 27, 2020, https://www.instagram.com/p/B9GAYqCpHor/.

Day 27 Ask Different Questions

1. Beth Moore, *The Quest* (Nashville: Lifeway, 2018), 13.
2. J. L. Hancock, *All the Questions in the Bible* (Oak Harbor, WA: Logos Research Systems, Inc., 1998), iii.
3. Hancock, *All the Questions in the Bible*.

Day 28 Let Life's Nor'easters Launch You Forward

1. Jennifer King Lindley, "What Is Resilience? Psychologists Explain How to Grow in Painful Moments," *Health*, June 25, 2020, https://www.health.com/condition/stress/how-to-heal-and-grow-from-our-toughest-moments.

Day 29 When You're in a Tight Space, Get Down Low

1. Matthew Henry, *Matthew Henry's Commentary on the Whole Bible: Complete and Unabridged in One Volume* (Peabody, MA: Hendrickson, 1994).
2. Henry, *Matthew Henry's Commentary on the Whole Bible*.

Day 30 Believe in Expiration Dates

1. Brower, *First Women*, 96.
2. Janet R. Osuch, "A Historical Perspective on Breast Cancer Activism: From Education and Support to Partnership in Scientific Research," *Journal of Women's Health*, March 2012, https://www.ncbi.nlm.nih.gov/pmc/articles/PMC3298674/.
3. Brower, *First Women*, 96.

4. Brower, *First Women*, 96.
5. Brower, *First Women*, 97.
6. John 19:30.
7. “Strong’s Lexicon: John 19:30,” Bible Hub, accessed June 1, 2020, https://biblehub.com/parallel/john/19-30.htm.

Day 31 What the Jonas Brothers and the Rest of Us Have in Common

1. “Happiness Continues: A Jonas Brothers Concert Film,” Amazon Prime video, 1:44 (0:40), 2020, https://www.amazon.com/gp/product/B0876MMHZY?autoplay=1&ref=dvm_us_api_cs_hud_pa_GWRD-singleCW&pf_rd_r=Q8DEEVZ6XPHWWN1N6MMH&pf_rd_p=e2f8fa8b-371f-466a-a14f-850b5d2c7966.
2. “Pruning Roses,” Wilson’s Garden Center, accessed October 14, 2020, https://gardencenterohio.com/rose/pruning-roses/.
3. Shelly Miller, @ShellyMillerWriter, Instagram caption, April 22, 2020, https://www.instagram.com/p/B_TDojIpZlH/.

Conclusion

1. Taken from Patricia Holbrook, “Uncomfortable Situations Are Used to Teach Us How to Soar,” *The Atlanta Journal-Constitution*, March 3, 2017.

KRISTEN STRONG, author of *Girl Meets Change* and *Back Roads to Belonging*, writes as a friend offering meaningful encouragement for each season of life so you can see it with more hope and less worry. She and her US Air Force veteran husband, David, have three children. Together this military family zigzagged across the country (and one ocean) several times before settling in Colorado Springs, Colorado. You can find her at kristenstrong.com, DaySpring's (in)courage, and on Instagram @kristenstrong and @girlmeetschange.

Connect with Kristen!

kristenstrong.com

@Kristen_Strong @chasingblueskies @kristenstrong

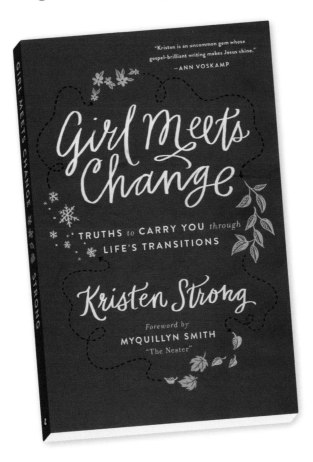

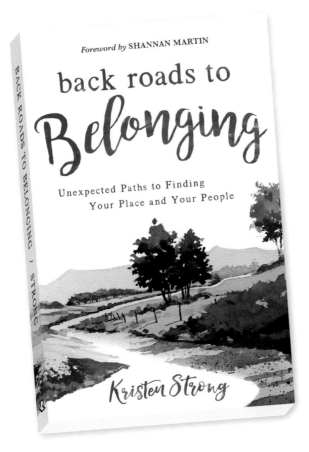